# VASES

# VASES

250 state-of-the-art designs

 Thames & Hudson

Agata Toromanoff

# Contents

006  **Introduction**

008  **Organic**

054  **Geometric**

094  **Architectonic**

128  **Sculptural**

172  **With a Twist**

238  **Designers A–Z**

254  **Picture Credits**

# Introduction

Floral art is having a revival. Ordinary florists' shops are transforming into floral design ateliers where arranging fragrant compositions becomes a high art form. Likewise, the design of vases is blooming. Contemporary designers increasingly push the boundaries of materials and technologies, making vases that are not only functional objects and desirable home accessories, but also important conceptual statements.

The vast range of contemporary vase designs presented here shows that there are no limits to what imaginative designers can make out of what is fundamentally a container for holding flowers. Some of their vases are astonishing displays of modern technical innovation; others explore traditional craft techniques with a contemporary twist, structural distortion or an unexpected pairing of materials. A few even appear to defy gravity. Modern vases are unconventional in every sense, wonderfully diverse in their aesthetic beauty and playful in materials and form.

The history of design includes many significant examples of state-of-the-art vases, but the scope and quality of those that we can admire (and acquire) today is unprecedented. This volume presents iconic 20th- and 21st-century designs from famous names such as Alvar Aalto, Ettore Sottsass, Tom Dixon and Zaha Hadid, but also investigates the contemporary scene with an exciting selection of emerging designers from the younger generation, which has seen a revival of interest in vase design. Inspired by the organic world, architectural elements, sculptural principles or geometry, all these designers translate their original visions into a variety of forms, keen to experiment and to blur the lines between design, art and architecture.

The vases in this book are contemporary works of art, worthy of inclusion in museum collections – and many actually are. As the beautiful images in these pages reveal, modern vases are both significant elements for décor and fascinating design objects.

**Opposite:**
**Tom Dixon • UK**
'Tank' vases • 2008

**Page 2:**
**Adrien Rovero • Switzerland**
'Sweets' vases • 2015

**Preceding pages:**
**ECAL / Decha Archjananun**
**for THINKK Studio •**
**Thailand**
'Weight Vases' for
Specimen Editions • 2011

ORGANIC

# Q&A with Anna Elzer Oscarson

**What makes a vase such an interesting design object for you?**

The vase is a combination of visual and functional object, which appeals to the designer in me. After designing patterns for a while, I wanted to deepen my skills in 3D shapes, and I also love flowers, so working with vases was a good match. The clay is so basic and fundamental, coming from the earth. But it is still a sophisticated, multifaceted and very beautiful material. It has a strong will. It challenges me and I just love it. The feeling when you hold it in your hands: at the start when it's flowing clay; then its fragility after casting; the crispy white after the first firing; and last, depending on which glaze you use, super smooth or matte. I also want to preserve the knowledge about ceramics that we have developed in Sweden over hundreds of years. This is why the collaboration has started with Porslinsfabriken, which has the necessary skills and resources. I'm particularly fascinated by how the designer and manufacturing process can interact to illuminate unexplored horizons.

**Your work is inspired by nature. Tell us more about how you translate stimulus from the natural world into a vase.**

What we have around us, whatever it is, influences and affects us. That's why I think it's important to be surrounded by beautiful things. Nature is a great source of inspiration: the rippling of the water's surface has inspired me to work with soft lines. It takes about 2 hours to travel to the porcelain factory by car. The landscape on the way is famous for its beauty and my glazes are inspired by these trips. You can really feel the landscape in the collection: the rolling oat fields, which change colour with the seasons from earthy brown to deep yellow; the vegetation and trees in all shades of green; and the little red cottages.

**Do you think that organic shapes are a better 'container' for flowers?**

The organic shapes appeal to me: they are beautiful and sensual and the flowers and the shapes interact with each other. When adding flowers I want the shapes from the vases somehow to continue.

**When designing a new vase are you more focused on creating a visually beautiful object or is the functional aspect most important?**

Scandinavian design is known for its focus on functionality, and my vases are, of course, easy to use, but for me visual beauty has just as much value. The objects should stand on their own, and be just as beautiful without flowers. When I design, I commute between these two parameters. The starting point for some shapes is the need for a certain size of vase and I let that control the design, but I never forget the importance of the visual beauty.

**A vase that you would like to design...?**

I would love to design a big floor vase and decorate it in various ways by hand.

These pages:
**Anna Elzer**
**Oscarson • Sweden**
'Dancing Dune'
collection · 2016–17

Sculptor **Aneta Regel** and ceramicist **Sandra Davolio** both design beautiful ceramic vases in organic forms inspired by nature. The traditional idea of a vase disappears in their designs, which look more like partially transformed elements from the natural world: rough pieces of rock, colourful coral or delicate exotic plants. Regel and Davolio are brilliant observers who uncover the beauty of organic shapes and immortalize their typically fragile, transient nature in solid materials. Finely detailed sculptural elements and skilfully textured surfaces capture the unique beauty of the natural objects evoked by each vase.

**Right:**
**Aneta Regel • Poland/UK**
'Raining Stones' vases
· 2017

**Opposite:**
**Sandra Davolio • Italy/Denmark**

Untitled stoneware vases
· 2005 (top left); 2014 (bottom left); 2008 (right)

Untitled porcelain vase
· 2017 (centre left)

**Sandra Davolio**

Inspired by shapes and textures found in the natural world, **The Haas Brothers** created their unique hand-thrown 'Accretion' series. Twin brothers Simon and Nikolai Haas developed the decorative technique for the series after observing the growth process of coral and tree fungus. Repeated applications of wet slip 'accrete' to imperfections in the dry clay body of the vessel, forming the fur- or petal-like growths. Other vases in the series incorporate brass, bronze, resins and polyurethane. Although entirely functional as vases, their inventive forms and artistic execution bring them closer to sculpture.

**The Haas Brothers • USA**

**Right:**
'Black Urchin Accretion'
vase · 2015

**Opposite:**
'Accretion' vase · 2013

Fluid torsion defines the shape of the translucent porcelain 'Wo' vase ('Wo' means a whirlwind in Chinese) designed by **Vincent Tordjman** for historic French firm Ligne Roset. Inspired by the power of nature, it evokes swirling water, as suggested by its name, which in turn references the object's function as a container for water. It was challenging to translate the designer's 3D model into a mould from which the vase could be manufactured, but the effect is truly poetic. The vase's wavelike shape not only seems to be moving in space, but also seems to change when viewed from different angles.

**Vincent Tordjman • France**
'Wo' vases for
Ligne Roset · 2017

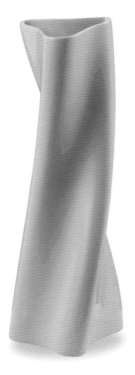

Claesson Koivisto Rune
• Sweden
'PO-0804' vase
for Cappellini · 2008

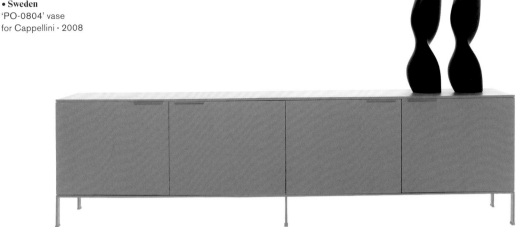

Claesson Koivisto Rune's elegant satin-finish ceramic vase (available in white or anthracite black) for Italian firm Cappellini embodies transformation, with a sleek body that seems to be in motion and invites one's gaze to move around it. 'When the composer Erik Satie created his *Gymnopédies* he described the small musical variation as a sculpture seen from different angles,' explain the architectural trio of the inspiration for the vase's distorted, gracefully twisting, organic form.

**Tom Dixon • UK**
'Warp' vases · 2016

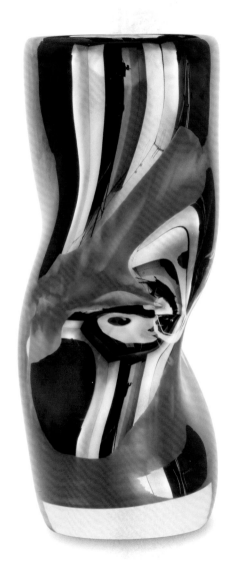

**Tom Dixon**'s 'Warp' vases display a similarly organic distortion in glass, amplified by a stunning iridescent finish inspired by the dazzling effect one can observe on a hummingbird's wing, peacock feathers or soap bubbles. The vases are created from mouth-blown glass cylinders that are deformed while the glass is in a molten state, making each one unique, and then re-fired at a high temperature with the applied finish.

The 'Scarabée' vase by **Jean-Baptiste Fastrez** for Moustache imitates the visual qualities of the scarab beetle it is named after. The two hard ceramic elements connected by an elastic band might look like part of a motorbike, but the vase's construction is actually inspired by the shape and arrangement of the beetle's jointed, winged carapace. The enamelled ceramic mimics the iridescent colours of the beetle's wings. 'The Scarabée vase', reads the studio's description, 'draws from certain contemporary or older fantastic mythologies,' also resembling the shape of canopic jars found in the tombs of ancient Egypt, where the scarab beetle was a symbol of rebirth associated with the sun-god Ra.

**Jean-Baptiste Fastrez • France** 'Scarabée' vase for Moustache · 2014

Jean-Baptiste Fastrez

Art glass pioneer **Göran Wärff** has been designing for Kosta Boda, the oldest glassworks in Sweden, since 1964. His designs are particularly famous for the beautiful way they interact with light, inspired by the optical phenomena of air vibrating on the horizon or wavering over hot desert sands. Curious combinations of colours in various hues are embodied in remarkable shapes such as his 'Mirage' and 'Vision Purple' vases.

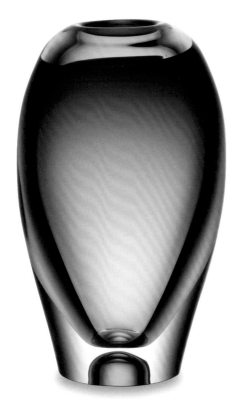

**Göran Wärff • Sweden**
'Mirage' vase (right) ·
'Vision Purple' vase (left),
both for Kosta Boda · undated

**Marcel Wanders** created the forms of his three porcelain 'Egg' vases for his retail brand Moooi by stuffing latex rubber condoms with hard-boiled eggs, yielding organic shapes reminiscent of clusters of eggs or bubbles. **Jomi Evers** made the moulds for his 'Elements' collection from balloons filled with water. In both collections, the elasticity of the materials lets the rounded shapes and physical properties of water and eggs dictate the form of the vases organically, creating playful and expressive pieces. Both designers leave the porcelain in its naturally white, unglazed state, focusing attention on the shape of the vase and its tactile sensation.

Below:
**Marcel Wanders**
• **Netherlands**
'Egg' vases for
Moooi · 1997

**Opposite:**
**Jomi Evers • Norway**
'Elements' vases · 2014

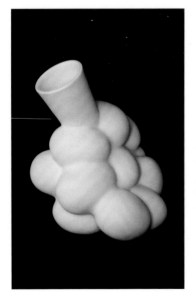  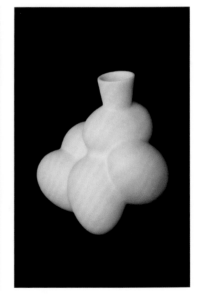

'One of the nice things about the "Elements" project is that I know how the balloon shape looks before the moulding process, but I can't predict the final result before slip-casting the porcelain. There has never been a physical original, just a transitory form, so it's really a magic moment when releasing the porcelain from the mould for the first time.'
Jomi Evers

The 'Tom Tom' collection by **Michal Fargo** includes several colourful vases made in porcelain. The concept was actually inspired by the shape of the bottom of a plastic soda bottle(!), but Fargo eventually used tomatoes to create more organic forms. The 'Tom Tom' vases, available in a range of related colours and shapes, are quite small and can hold either tiny or single flowers, but also work nicely in a group.

**Ted Muehling** explored the shapes of birds' eggs in a diverse collection of exquisite minimalist vases for historic traditional German porcelain firm Porzellan Manufaktur Nymphenburg. The precision and smoothness of the forms are striking. 'I try to restrict my vocabulary of shape by abstracting forms from nature and transforming them with the aim of creating objects that function just as well as they look,' explains Muehling. The smallest vase in the series, 'Goose Egg', is available in matte gold brushed with 24-carat fine gold, bringing understated luxury and timeless elegance to the classic form. Varying in size and colour, the vases in the collection can be displayed singly or grouped together in decorative arrangements.

**Ted Muehling • USA**
'Egg' vases (above, left
and right) · 'Goose Egg'
vase with 24-carat gold (left),
all for Nymphenburg · 2000

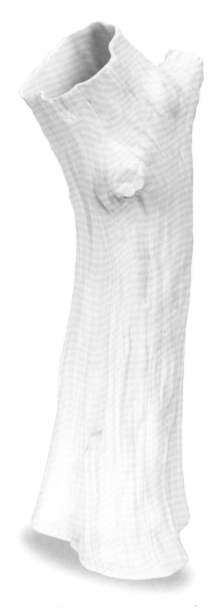

Trees and branches appeal to designers' imaginations. From a practical point of view the shape is perfect as a container for flowers; from an artistic perspective it plays with the idea of blossoming trees. The 'Branch' vase, another design by **Ted Muehling** for Porzellan Manufaktur Nymphenburg, is astonishing for its high degree of detail. The porcelain mimics perfectly the nuanced wrinkles of tree bark, while its irregular shape echoes the form of a tree trunk. Only the white colour makes the vase more resemble a statue than part of a living tree. **Richard Woods**'s 'Tree Trunk' vase for Danish firm HAY doesn't imitate a tree trunk naturalistically, but reinterprets its shape playfully, in two- or three-branched models decorated with stylized hand-painted patterns. Flowers can be placed in the branches as well as the trunk section, allowing more possibilities for arrangement.

**Left:**
**Ted Muehling • USA**
'Branch' vase for
Nymphenburg · 2014

**Opposite:**
**Richard Woods • UK**
'Tree Trunk ' vase for
HAY · 2015

These handmade vases by Melbourne-based studio **KLEIN&SCHÖN** are one-of-a-kind pieces made of polymer clay with a resin-coated interior. 'Sea Slug', 'Tall' and 'Short' vases are striking in their formal simplicity, which highlights the symphony of interestingly applied colours. Splashes of red, lilac, aqua, golden yellow, baby pink or navy are smeared irregularly onto the white background, making the vases resemble cross-sections of banded stone.

The 'Blueware' vases made by London-based studio **Glithero** are part of a beautiful series inspired by early 20th-century cyanotype photography. Founders Tim Simpson and Sarah van Gameren decorate their bulb-like earthenware vases by using photosensitive pigments to capture impressions of botanical specimens – including weeds collected on London pavements. The plants are pressed, dried and fixed to a vase coated in Prussian blue, which is then exposed to ultraviolet light. The plants block the light, leaving crisp white silhouettes while the surrounding areas turn blue.

Glithero • UK
'Blueware' vases · 2010

Famous for employing asymmetrical wavy shapes, **Alvar Aalto** was fascinated by the sinuous lines seen in the organic world. His iconic 'Aalto' vase, also known as the 'Savoy' vase, designed in 1936, is still one of the most popular glass objects worldwide. Its undulating lines echo the Finnish landscape, which is rich in lakes, and also reference the designer's own surname, which means 'waves'.

This page:
**Alvar Aalto • Finland**
'Aalto' vases for Karhula-Iittala · 1936

'I usually sketch products by folding and building shapes in paper. It's an interesting process that often gives you a different end result than you first intended.' Clara von Zweigbergk

**Clara von Zweigbergk**'s interest in the qualities of paper yielded the sinusoid lines of her 'Iris' vase for HAY. The sharp, regular edges of the collection, executed in very thin matte-finish porcelain (handcrafted by Arita in Japan), are the result of her experiments with paper. The designer tried folding paper of various weights into rounded shapes to imagine the vases. The paper's fragility and suppleness has been perfectly reproduced in porcelain, and paper is also evoked by the soft colour palette.

**Clara von Zweigbergk**
• **Sweden**
'Iris' vase for HAY · 2017

Vases from **Design by O** and **Emmanuel Babled** evoke water and its fluid properties in radically different materials and forms. 'Cascade' by Design by O for Ligne Roset is a set of three white ceramic vases in graduated sizes, with softly rounded organic contours. The three vases can be used individually or stacked together to resemble a series of waterfalls; flowers can then be placed at three different levels. Babled's hand-blown 'Pyros' vases are decorated with overlapping spots of coloured glass that are 'thrown' against the vase, forming one-of-a-kind patterns reminiscent of the spatter of raindrops against a window.

**This page:**
**Design by O • France**
'Cascade' vases for
Ligne Roset · 2007

**Opposite:**
**Emmanuel Babled**
**• Portugal**
'Pyros' vase for
Venini · 2016

'Working in the furnace often means seizing the moment: it takes an instant to crystallize materials and colours.' Emmanuel Babled

The earth, its processes and geology intrigue vase designers. The 'Erosion' vase from **Studio Wieki Somers** explores the mechanism of the earth being worn down by wind, water or glacial ice. Made of bull's-eye glass, the vase has been produced in a limited edition of 99 pieces. **Ferréol Babin**, who feels a need to be surrounded by nature when he works, was inspired by raised elements of earth in creating his ceramic 'Mountain' vases. Finally, the 'Stone' vase by brothers **Ronan and Erwan Bouroullec** translates geological structures into a curiously organic yet geometric shape rendered in enamelled porcelain for one of the studio's early projects, which was commissioned by the Délégation aux Arts Plastiques of the French Ministry of Culture.

**Studio Wieki Somers**
• **Netherlands**
'Erosion' vase for
Thomas Eyck · 2016

**Above:**
**Ferréol Babin • France**
'Mountain' vases
for Pulpo · 2017

**Left:**
**Ronan and Erwan**
**Bouroullec • France**
'Stone' ('Caillou')
vase · 2002

**Ferréol Babin / Ronan and Erwan Bouroullec**

Above and opposite:
**Studio Furthermore** • UK
'Replica' vases · 2017

'Replica' is a collection of vases and other vessels showcasing an experimental manufacturing method developed by **Studio Furthermore**. Designers Marina Dragomirova and Iain Howlett's 'lost foam' replication process works with both ceramic and aluminium alloy materials. It involves making a foam original that is then burned away either by molten metal or clay fired in a kiln, leaving behind a precise replica (hence the name) of the bubbled foam in either metal or ceramic. The designers say that they were inspired by geological processes they observed on a visit to Iceland, where 'foamy lava rocks and cooled magma debris decorate an alien landscape of volcanoes, geysers and icebergs'.

**Anna Elzer Oscarson** says that her work is 'inspired by the ripples on the water's surface, the shifting open spaces, where the boundary between dazzling skies and rich soil becomes blurred'. The subtle lines and ridges decorating her 'Dancing Dune' vases and tableware evoke the patterns of sand dunes shaped by water and wind. The 'Dusty Diamonds' line, on the other hand, is adorned with crystalline patterns reminiscent of the sparkle of natural gems or frost on a windowpane. Her practice involves a combination of contemporary 3D computer modelling and traditional craftsmanship, as the vases are manufactured by historic Swedish firm Porslinsfabriken i Lidköping.

Anna Elzer Oscarson
• Sweden

**Above:**
'Dancing Dune'
collection · 2016–17

**Right:**
'Dusty Diamonds'
vase · 2010–11

**Anna Elzer Oscarson**

The unpretentious and natural, slightly irregular shapes of the 'Botanica' vase collection from studio **R7B** (design duo Mette Bache and Barbara Bendix Becker) are great additions to a cosy interior. Available in varying shapes and sizes, the vases resemble flower bulbs, with glazes in a muted palette of interesting hues. The bottoms of the vases incorporate furrows that are designed to support stems and make flower arranging easier.

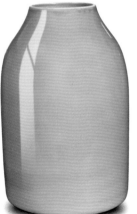

This page:
**R7B • Denmark**
'Botanica' vases for
Kähler Design · undated

**R7B**

Architect **Zaha Hadid**'s creations always amaze. Made of Carrara marble, Hadid's 'Tau' series of vases for Italian stone company Citco feature intricate pleats 'expressing the formal complexity of natural growth systems', according to the designer. The contrast of fragile flower petal forms with the solidity of the material makes a strong visual statement. All the 'Tau' vases (available in five different sizes and shapes) were created using a milling machine that carved away pieces from a solid block following a digital model. The form of Hadid's lacquered polyethylene 'Flow' vase is also reminiscent of flower petals, as well as of the movement of water. Developed with Patrik Schumacher for Italian furniture and lighting firm Serralunga, 'Flow' was an experiment in combining 3D modelling techniques and rotational moulding technology, with the goal of creating a vase that is also a sculpture.

**Zaha Hadid • Iraq/UK**

**Left and above:**
'Tau' vases for
Citco · 2014

**Opposite:**
'Flow' vases for
Serralunga · 2006–07

**Bold • France**
'Poilu' vases for Aybar
Gallery · 2016

The experimental 'Poilu' collection was created by design studio **Bold** to push the boundaries of advanced technology. The first limited edition comprises three different vases, which are truly organic as they are made from natural fibres such as wood, bamboo or coconut fibre that are 3D printed, using innovative techniques developed by the studio for generating and implanting 'hair'. The resulting vases have intriguing forms that are superficially rough and organic, yet surprisingly regular in their execution, which, together with their innovative materials, gives them a unique appearance.

These vases, conceived by artist **Tomáš Libertíny**, were intended by their makers to hold not flower stems, but pollen and nectar. Constructed of wax by honey bees, in what can be viewed as a fully organic reinterpretation of computer-aided 3D printing processes, each piece in the collection of nine vessels was built on a vase-shaped 'scaffold', which was then removed once the hive of 40,000 bees had finished their meticulous comb-building. Libertíny created 'The Honeycomb Vase' to explore his lifelong fascination with the beauty and intelligence of nature. He has since developed the technique to produce other vessels and sculptural works 'made by bees'.

**Tomáš Libertíny**
• **Slovakia/Netherlands**
'The Honeycomb Vase'
· 2005 (conception) /
2006–2010 (realization)

'Luft' means 'air' in Swedish and is the fundamental natural element that inspired the silhouettes of **Luca Nichetto**'s vases for Swedish firm Fogia. Although their basic shapes resemble hot-air balloons about to lift off, their solid, heavy bases keep them anchored firmly on the ground. The vases are hand-blown from Murano glass in small editions of only 33 numbered pieces for each size. The shallow ribs and folds create subtle patterns that work well with the natural grey and amber hues of the glass.

'The wood represents the roots in the soil and the glass the airy treetop, as it stands in nature, altogether creating a vase that combines a solid and rooted base with a light and divine top.'

Thomas Bentzen

These vases feature natural glass colours and rounded, jar-like forms. The 'Elevated' vase, designed by **Thomas Bentzen** for Muuto, is inspired by trees: the hand-blown glass jar, representing the airy foliage, rests on a bowl made of polished ash wood, representing the solid trunk rooted in soil. When flowers are placed in the nearly transparent vase, they appear to be suspended. In contrast, **Héctor Serrano**'s 'Natura Jars' for La Mediterranea, made of recycled glass in green, amber and red, are fairly opaque, with flower stems only barely visible through the glass. The wooden element (in this case, a cork lid) rests on the top of the glass bases, and allows them to be used either as storage jars or as decorative vases.

Dechem Studio
• Czech Republic
'Bandaska' vases
for Ligne Roset · 2016

The smooth shapes and soft colours of these mouth-blown glass vases evoke the natural world. 'Bandaska' vases from Prague-based **Dechem Studio** are made of Bohemian glass blown into wooden moulds, a traditional technique that is difficult to master. The diluted, unevenly distributed pigments in the glass give a shadowy, organic effect. Jelena Schou Nordentoft and Ditte Reckweg of **Stilleben** etch their 'Omaggio Glass' vases with regular yet subtle stripes. The 'Form' vases from Danish firm **Lyngby Porcelæn** please the eye with their nicely rounded shapes and precisely executed rims.

**Right and far right:**
**Stilleben • Denmark**
'Omaggio Glass' vases
for Kähler Design · 2016

**Below:**
**Lyngby Porcelæn • Denmark**
'Form' vases · 2016

**Stilleben / Lyngby Porcelæn**

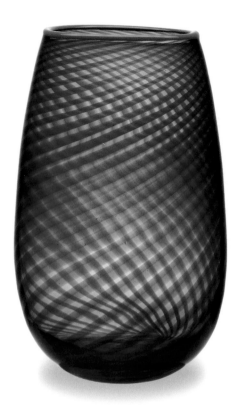

Glass artist **Bertil Vallien** and designer **Marie-Aurore Stiker-Metral** both experiment with stunning shades of blue in their vases, reminiscent of the most intense hues of sky and sea. While Vallien is fascinated by water and its currents (he begins every day with a dip in the river!), the decoration of Stiker-Metral's vase was inspired by the 'fish-scale' armour worn by Japanese samurai. In order to obtain the ornamental motif at the top of the neck, the glass is hand-blown, moulded and then cut so that it interacts remarkably with light.

**Above:**
**Bertil Vallien • Sweden**
'Red Rim' vase for
Kosta Boda · undated

**Right:**
**Marie-Aurore Stiker-Metral**
**• France**
'Samurai' vase for
Ligne Roset · 2014

Originally a lawyer, legendary Italian glassmaker **Paolo Venini** decided instead to devote himself to design in the early 1930s. Although he often worked in collaboration with other designers and artists, he personally mastered the hands-on art of glassmaking, founded a glassmaking firm and created his own remarkable collections, promoting and reviving traditional Murano glass techniques. The elegant 'Incisi' collection dates from 1956, but its design is timeless, with five different silhouettes made of translucent Murano glass. After the glass has cooled, the surface is engraved using a grinder made of stone. Their silky, fluid, organic shapes resemble uncut precious stones.

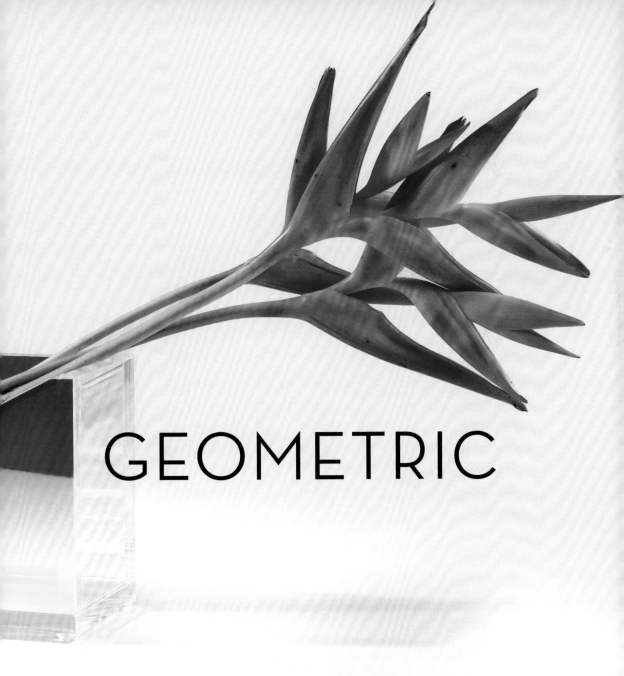

GEOMETRIC

# Q&A with Joogii Design
— Juliette and Diogo Felippelli

**Your 'French Touch' collection includes a coffee table, side table, desk objects, a chair and, last but not least, a vase. The vase is not an obvious choice to accompany the others, so why did you decide to have it in the series?**

I think the decision was two-fold: we wanted to try our hand at designing home accessories and to offer another price point within the collection. From our experience in designing accessories we've found that sometimes the smaller objects pose the biggest challenge.

Because there is so little space to play with, details have to be carefully considered and we need to exercise even more restraint to achieve the most simple expression of our concept.

**Is a vase a challenging object to design?**

Yes. In making the vases as part of a collection that includes furniture, they had to speak the same design language, but offer a completely different function. We wanted to create a design that was not only beautiful, but one that could also

display flora in a very original way, hence the asymmetrical cut of the mouth of our 'Thomas' vase (*see opposite*) and the deep V-cut in our 'Guy-Man' vase (*see preceding pages*). We thought of these cuts as a 'reveal' (a term used in furniture or millwork design) in which designers add a metal edge or band for an extra touch of detail. In this case, we cut away from our design to reveal more of the flower within the vase to create a sense of intrigue.

**Your collection is defined by geometric shapes, exposed edges and interlocking elements. At the same time, geometry is a perfect stage for playing with the most beautiful hues (each piece is coated with a hand-applied dichroic film that changes saturation depending on the light). This effect is particularly poetic in the vases, which also interact with the colours of flowers. What was your inspiration for the collection?**

Our inspiration was the dichroic film itself. It reminded us of our disco-filled nights on the dance floor (we actually met on one in Rio de Janeiro and DJed together for many years) and we wanted to evoke those feelings of being uninhibited.

**Right:**
**Joogii Design • USA**
'Thomas' vase · 2016

**Preceding pages:**
**Joogii Design • USA**
'French Touch' vases:
'Thomas' (left) · 'Guy-Man'
(right) · 2016

The beauty of the film is that it interacts with everything around it and changes colour constantly – with the time of day and with any adjacent objects and colours – so it's never static. The interplay of the colours of the vase with those of the flowers within it adds to the multi-dimensional beauty of the object.

**The contrast between the geometric forms of your vases and the more organic forms of the flowers is** very interesting. If you continue designing vases, will you explore geometry further?

Yes. Geometry is one of our starting points for our projects, along with colour and materiality. We are always looking for the next great material or collection of materials that we can dynamically incorporate into our projects.

The 'Stockholm Aquatic' and 'Stockholm Horizon' vases from Swedish design duo **Bernadotte & Kylberg** for Danish design brand Stelton are inspired by the nuanced palette of blues reflected in the Baltic Sea and around the Stockholm archipelago, which the designers observed throughout the year. The vases' smoothly formed geometric shapes encourage a spectacular, ephemeral and constantly shifting interplay of the glazed patterns with real reflected light from their surroundings.

**Bernadotte & Kylberg**
• Sweden

**Below:**
'Stockholm Aquatic'
vase for Stelton · 2015

**Opposite:**
'Stockholm Horizon'
vase for Stelton · 2015

The round-edged rectangular shapes of **Adrien Rovero**'s 'Sweets' collection were informed by a type of candy. The vases are coloured in sugary pastel hues and the designer even presents them on a plate, as if serving candy. The accompanying 'plate' bases on which the vases stand not only have an aesthetic role, but are also the perfect way to collect fallen petals.

**Adrien Rovero • Switzerland**
'Sweets' vases · 2015

'The idea behind the product is to try to activate an unexpected sense in the objects, the taste. How will it be if you see an object you want to eat? What would happen?' Adrien Rovero

Noé Duchaufour-Lawrance
• France
'Marie' vase (right) ·
'Antoinette' vase (left),
both for Ligne Roset · 2016

The beauty of the 'Marie' and 'Antoinette'
vases designed by **Noé Duchaufour-Lawrance**
is the result of a long manufacturing process.
The enamelled faience requires no less than
three firings and the bicolour crackle finish is
technically the outcome of overcooking. Glossy
ovals of pastel pink subtly accentuate the
sophisticated soft rectangular shapes.

Anders Arhøj's 'Unico' vase and **Nousaku**'s 'Tama' designs are interesting variations on the sphere. The perfectly round, unadorned geometric form invites experimentation with beautiful materials – Japanese-inspired glazed ceramic by Danish designer Arhøj and solid brass by century-old Japanese metalwork firm Nousaku. Arhøj's glaze is applied randomly on the surface to give a feeling of three-dimensional depth. The beauty of the material is also the focus of 'Tama' (which means 'sphere' in Japanese) – each piece is hand-polished by craftsmen. These perfect spheres are ideal bases for simple flower compositions.

Below:
Nousaku • Japan
'Tama' vases · 2013

Above:
Anders Arhøj • Denmark
'Unico' vase for Kähler
Design · 2015

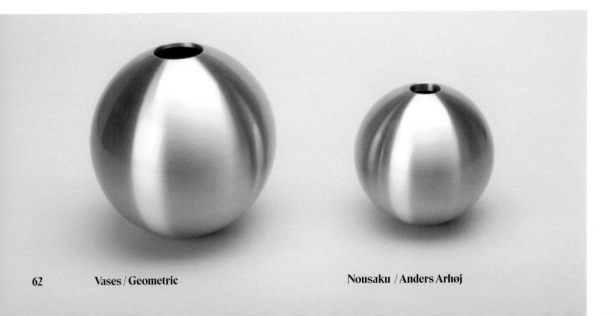

Vases / Geometric

Nousaku / Anders Arhøj

This page:
**Dimorestudio • Italy**
'Equilibri Collection' vases
for Bitossi Ceramiche ·
2016–17

Emiliano Salci and Britt Moran, the founders
of Milanese interior design studio **Dimorestudio**,
were commissioned to look into the archives
of Italian ceramic firm Bitossi Ceramiche and
find ways to reinterpret the company's hallmark
techniques with new designs. Their resulting
'Equilibri Collection' focuses on ceramic teamed
with brass: a series of striking rectangular vases
that feature blocks of rich pigment colour and
look almost architectural in form.

Simplicity meets modern lines in the minimalist
'Fall 2017' collection hand-sculpted by **Tina
Frey**. The vases in the series are unadorned
white porcelain, putting the focus entirely
on the precision of their shapes and sublime
functionality. **Skogsberg & Smart** (Magnus
Skogsberg and Mimmi Smart) also follow the
minimalist path with their 'Hurricane' collection,
which is hand-blown by world-renowned
Bohemian glass artisans. The plain, reflective
coating on the 'Hurricane Lily' vase emphasizes
its simple, tall, elegant and functional shape.

**Above:**
**Tina Frey • USA**
'Fall 2017' collection · 2017

**Opposite:**
**Skogsberg & Smart •**
**Sweden/UK**
'Hurricane Lily' vase · 2009

Each vase by **Phil Cuttance** is individually produced by casting resin into a simple handmade mould, which is later manipulated by hand to create each object's form before casting. As a result of this process, every piece is unique and the designer also numbers them or names them individually (if you order one from the designer, you can even ask for a message of up to 20 characters to be cast into the piece).

**Phil Cuttance**
• **New Zealand/UK**

**This page:**
'Herringbone' vases · 2016

**Opposite:**
'Faceture Straight Tall'
vase · 2013

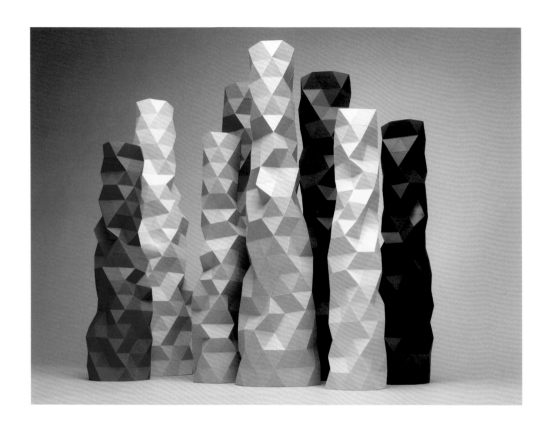

'I am interested in creating objects whose form, often detailed and visually complex, belies the hand-made, lo-fi processes by which they are created. On closer inspection the objects often reveal small imperfections, which are a result of the process and communicate the handmade nature of the piece.'

Phil Cuttance

Phil Cuttance

Clarity, minimalism and classic lines are the guiding principles of Berit Lüdecke and Heiko Büttner of **SNUG.STUDIO**. Their inventive DIY cardboard vase is easy and quick to assemble. All you have to do is to fold a pre-cut and creased sheet of cardboard to create the multifaceted geometric body of the vase, which is available in two different sizes and three colours, and then place it over a bottle or a glass of water.

SNUG.STUDIO • Germany
'Snug.Vase' · 2012

'We always follow our intention and we have high ambitions for what we do. Everything that goes into production we would like to have for ourselves.' SNUG.STUDIO

Above and right:
**Jean-Christophe
Clair • France**
'Totem' vases for
Roche Bobois · 2017

Above:
**Ilot Ilov • Germany**
'Geo-Cut' vases · 2017

Austere geometry doesn't have to be boring: interpreted imaginatively, it can result in playful vases. **Ilot Ilov**'s set of three 'Geo-Cut' vases are made of powder-coated aluminium and available in black, white or blue. Each of the monochromatic shapes is designed to hold a different type of bouquet. **Jean-Christophe Clair** features combinations of bright colours and tiny speckles on the matt enamel finish of his playful geometric 'Totem' vases, which – despite their machine-like precision – are actually hand-turned red clay earthenware below the surface.

The contrast between the geometric impact of sharp lines with the delicate, organic nature of flowers interests **Antonio Facco**. His 'Duo' vase for Cappellini consists of two interlocking elements in black or white, with holes that allow the same flower to pass through both parts, in effect tying them even more closely together. The design is modular, which allows varied arrangements to be created.

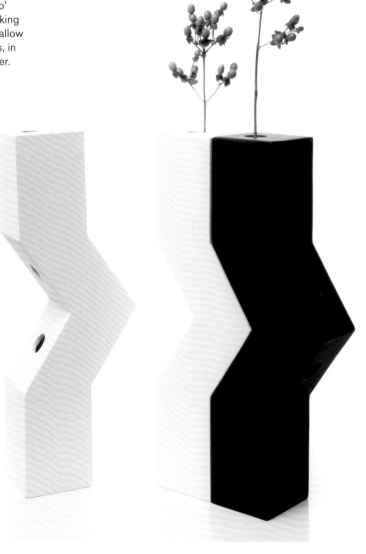

**Antonio Facco • Italy**
'Duo' vase for Cappellini
· 2014

**Antonio Facco**

Vases / Geometric

71

'Glass is a material that likes round shapes. When hot it flows like honey and does not like to be pulled into a very precise geometric shape. By developing the strict shape we are reaching the limits of the material.' Ronan and Erwan Bouroullec

Brothers **Ronan and Erwan Bouroullec**'s collection of mouth-blown glass containers for Finnish firm Iittala juxtapose strong materials and sharp lines with the delicate flowers they hold. 'Ruutu' means diamond or square in Finnish. Available in five different sizes, in a palette of watercolour hues, the modular collection paradoxically explores the nature of glass by forcing it into an unnaturally geometric form.

This page:
**Ronan and Erwan Bouroullec • France**
'Ruutu' vases
for Iittala · 2014

The surface of a vase can be geometrically textured to enhance the play of light. While **Patricia Urquiola** applies a quilted, waffle-like pattern, **Vanessa Mitrani** uses bubbles and circles. Urquiola's 'Matelassé' vase for Kartell is made of acrylic glass, a high-quality plastic. 'Geometric Circle' for Roche Bobois showcases Mitrani's skilful, creative glassblowing. Regularly applied geometric motifs soften the sturdiness of the material and give the vessel a unique form, enhanced by its rounded, decorative framework.

Above:
Patricia Urquiola
• Spain/Italy
'Matelassé' vases
for Kartell · 2011

Right:
Vanessa Mitrani • France
'Geometric Circle' vases
for Roche Bobois · 2015

Carving on glass can create truly stunning geometric patterns and visual effects. **Nicolas Triboulot**'s 'Eye Collection' vases (available in both rectangular and oval shapes) for Baccarat celebrate light and its magical qualities. Exterior horizontal and interior vertical cuts create a symphony of shades when the vase interacts with external light, and the intensity of the texture seems to set the surface into motion. Similarly, the 'Cupcake' vase by **Anna Ehrner** for Kosta Boda has a simple shape adorned with regular vertical cuts to obtain a shimmering effect. Made in a range of subtle yet expressive colours, the vase resembles a pleated, ethereal fabric.

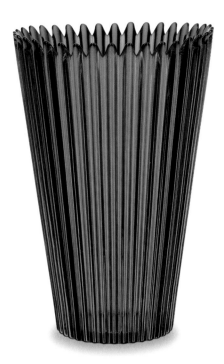

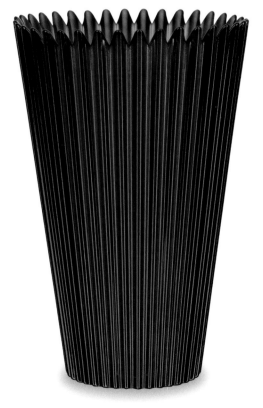

**This page:**
**Anna Ehrner • Sweden**
'Cupcake' vases for
Kosta Boda · undated

**Opposite:**
**Nicolas Triboulot • France**
'Eye Collection Oval'
vases (above) for Baccarat
· 2018; and 'Eye Collection
Rectangular' vases (above,
far right, and below)
for Baccarat · 2016

Inspired by the shape of emerald-cut diamonds, the 'Jewel' vases from **Louise Roe** come in three sizes. While the smallest model can hold only a single flower, the largest is perfect for a bouquet. Their sophisticated simplicity of form plays well with the refined colour tones selected for the series. The semi-transparent glass deepens in colour around the softened edges of the otherwise starkly geometric vase, emphasizing its square lines and making it a very elegant frame for displaying flowers.

**Louise Roe • Denmark**
'Jewel' vases · 2015

**Nendo • Japan**
'Patchwork' vases
for Lasvit · 2013

**Nendo** takes handling glass even further by exploring the fine cutting techniques for which Bohemian glass is famous. The studio's collection of vases for Czech glassware brand Lasvit look like a transparent patchwork quilt. The vases are made by reheating objects already decorated with traditional cut-glass patterns, slicing them into pieces and then reassembling them into a single large vase. As with a patchwork quilt, this process of piecing together elements with various patterns creates multilayered, one-of-a-kind objects.

Ceramicist **Milan Pekař** tested many types of glaze before he became fascinated with crystal glazes. Mixing different oxides and ingredients plus skilful temperature adjustment during the firing results in endless visual variations. The pure geometric forms of the vases, with intentionally simple shapes and proportions, make a perfect canvas for these wildly colourful and intricate glazes. 'My goal is to show this colourful blast of crystals but not to go over the top,' says Pekař.

This page:
**Milan Pekař • Czech Republic**
'Crystalline' vases · 2015

**Milan Pekař**

'Geometric' doesn't have to mean simple forms or sharp edges. Italian design legend **Ettore Sottsass** experimented with varying proportions and compositions to create playful shapes, even in a material as challenging as glass. Sottsass not only invented original structures, but also employed strong colours. His vases were manufactured using the opal glassmaking technique, which was invented in 15th-century Murano to imitate porcelain. In the spherical components of these vases, milk-white opal glass is overlain by transparent bright-coloured glass for incredible richness and depth.

**Ettore Sottsass • Italy**

**Left:**
'Puzzle' vases
for Venini · 2003

**Below:**
'Yemen' vase
for Venini · 1984

**Ettore Sottsass**

These pages:
Tom Dixon • UK
'Tank' vases · 2008

**Tom Dixon** plays with proportions and compositions to achieve strong but playful shapes, even in a material as challenging as glass. The minimalist 'Tank' collection, which includes several vases, combines clear glass with hand-painted copper bands. While these vases may remind one of lab equipment, they are a perfect base for colourful flowers.

Simple shapes and amazing colours are at the core of the 'Hot Spots' series of faceted porcelain vases by **Christine Rathmann** for Rosenthal. The vases change appearance depending on the angle of viewing and the amount of light, and in certain types of lighting almost appear to rotate, as the spectrum-like arrangement of harmonious colour gradations invites the eye to move around the vase. As manufacturer Rosenthal states, 'the vase series is like a dance of colours'.

**Christine Rathmann**
• **Germany**
'Hot Spots' vases
for Rosenthal · 2016

These angular, transparent vases act as prisms to harmonize light with plants and flowers. Inspired by Impressionist painters' treatment of light, **Hattern** produced its 'Mellow Collection' of blurred, acrylic rectangular vases with colour gradations that are simply mesmerizing.

The transparent, crystalline 'Acrilic' vases by **Tomoko Mizu** for Cappellini create a dialogue between pure geometric forms and touches of sharp-edged colour. The hallmarks of the 'French Touch' collection from **Joogii Design** are exposed edges, interlocking elements and prismatic effects. Milled by a CNC machine, the pieces, including two vases, are coated with a hand-applied dichroic film, which changes hue and saturation depending on the intensity of light.

This page:
**Moreno Ratti • Italy**
'Suspended Collection'
(Collezione Sospesa) vases
for Marmo Trilogy · 2016

**Moreno Ratti**

Marble is a classic but technically demanding material from which to make a vase. **Moreno Ratti**'s 'Suspended Collection' of three vases is made of the waste material from coring Carrera marble, and suspended in the same transparent resin that is used industrially to stabilize the quarried stone before it is cut into slabs. His softly rounded marble vessels seem miraculously suspended in a sharp-edged transparent cube, giving an illusion of weightlessness. The tubular 'Duet' vase by **Michaël Verheyden** also juxtaposes marble with a different material, in this case a thick ring of brass at the base of the vase. Both designs feature marble in simple, geometric forms with clean lines, creating a striking contrast between the massiveness of the stone vessel and the delicacy of the flowers it holds.

**Right:**
**Michaël Verheyden**
**• Belgium**
'Duet' vase · 2012

**Michaël Verheyden**

The striking 'Block Double' vase by **Apparatus Studio** comprises brass tubes (with removable, rounded 'capsule' lids) sunk into a cast crystal block. This is achieved via a special technique of pouring molten Swedish barium crystal glass into graphite moulds, textured to make the cooled glass look like a block of ice. The optical illusion of the tubes floating freely creates an imaginative display for individual stems. **Studio Wieki Somers**'s 'Deepwater' vase plays with perception in similar ways. The vase consists of a sealed slab-like glass tank filled with black oil floating on water. According to the studio, 'This refers to the oil that originates on the bottom of our oceans…disrupted through human actions.' Flower stems are placed in a test tube that is embedded in the block, creating the illusion that they are drowning in the oil.

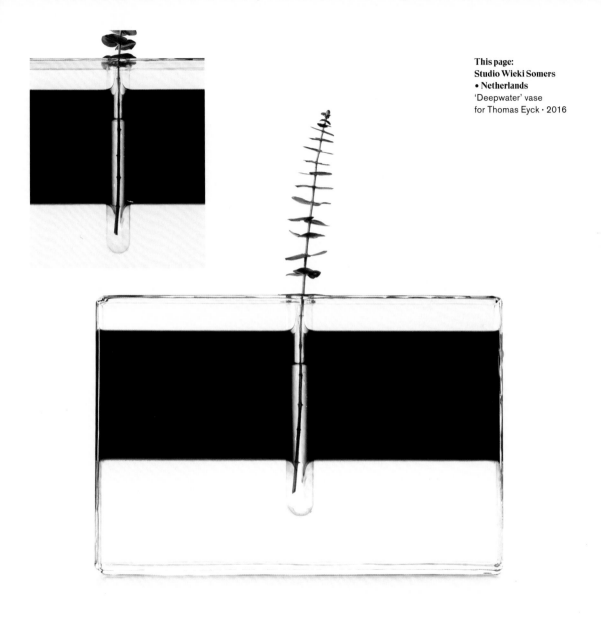

This page:
**Studio Wieki Somers**
**• Netherlands**
'Deepwater' vase
for Thomas Eyck · 2016

A tube-shaped vase typically holds only a single stem, but the basic tube form can be multiplied in unusual compositions. **Ronan and Erwan Bouroullec**'s modular 'Nuage' vases for Vitra each consist of eight tubular cavities grouped in shapes that, according the manufacturer, are 'reminiscent of a cloud', and have an anodized aluminium finish that deepens the interplay of light and shadow. Flower stems can be arranged in 'Nuage' vases of various heights to form forest-like displays. **Pierre Charpin**'s 'Triplo' vases for Venini involve three blown-glass tubes, each in a different colour, bound together with elastic to create a rainbow of light effects.

**Kateryna Sokolova**
• **Ukraine**
'Suprematic' vases for
Postformula Craft · 2017

The imaginative 'Suprematic' vases created by **Kateryna Sokolova** are inspired by the work of early 20th-century Russian avant-garde artist Kazimir Malevich and named for the abstract art movement he promoted. Suprematism emphasized the use of geometric forms and a limited range of colours to convey strong emotions, and Sokolova's interesting compositions reflect this fascination with geometric forms and simple colour palettes. She wants the geometric shapes that adorn her vases to be more than mere decorations; they are forms carefully chosen to stimulate and challenge the eye.

ARCHITECTONIC

# Q&A with Guillaume Delvigne

**Among the objects you have designed are armchairs, tables, make-up palettes, glasses, carpets and lamps to mention but a few. There are also several inventive vases. How did designing them differ from creating other works in your portfolio?**

I have a special affection for designing vases – they have always inspired me. My first project was a vase, back in 2004. For me it doesn't really differ from creating something else, as it is more or less the same creative process.

**Your vases can be seen both as unique objects and as vessels for flowers. Some have complex structures, others playful concepts. Which is at the core of your creative process: form or function?**

Most of the time form takes the lead in my research. This is more exaggerated when I'm designing a vase because the functionality of the object is easy, so I am able to concentrate on its form and concept. I generally put a lot of attention into the proportions, definition and precision of the shapes. This is what I like most in my job.

**Do you design a vase with particular flowers in mind?**

Not really, apart from particular cases where it is part of the initial brief or if I have a very special idea in mind. Usually I try to follow my intuition and once I've got a good idea, it leads to how you put the flowers in the vase and which kind of flowers will suit it.

**After exploring numerous materials, techniques and formal solutions, how would you describe the main challenge in designing a vase?**

It is always a big challenge, like when you try to design a chair: almost everything has already been done. At the same time, designing a vase feels like less of a heavy responsibility than designing a chair because there is no comfort issue. A vase is more a symbolic object than something you really need in your life, but it can also carry a lot of poetry. Having said that, we have to be careful because the border can be very thin between an interesting object and a vulgar decorative gadget.

**What is the source of inspiration and starting point for a new vase?**

It is always hard for me to understand where my inspiration comes from because it is something so diffuse. It can come from anything – an industrial detail or a vegetal shape – but for me it often starts with a desire to combine different materials. I like to take that exercise as a good excuse to deepen my personal research. You can really put a lot of your vision into a vase project.

Below:
Guillaume Delvigne
• France
'Deneb' vase for
Specimen · 2010

**Karen Chekerdjian** explores architectural forms in her 'OBJECT 03 XYZ' vases. Interested in the interconnection between function, form and meaning, Chekerdjian experiments with materials and combines contemporary patterns and designs with traditional workmanship. Made from highly polished copper sheets soldered together so seamlessly that they resemble folded paper, these limited-edition vases interact with the light and walls of the surrounding space, making their unusual shapes seem to shift.

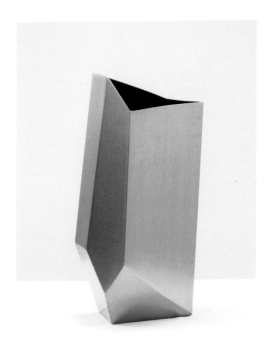

These pages:
Karen Chekerdjian
• Lebanon
'OBJECT 03 XYZ'
vases · 2009

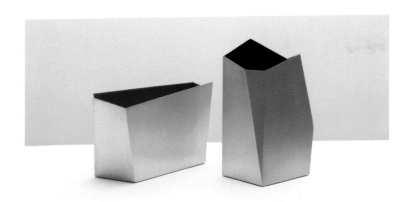

**Tadao Ando • Japan**
'Ando' vase for Venini
· 2011

**Tadao Ando**'s eponymous vase for Venini is a limited edition of 90 art pieces made of hand-blown glass and available in clear, red or blue. Drawing on architectural principles, the vase consists of three separate elements, each of which is a triangular column with curved surfaces whose unusual shape results from inverting isosceles triangles between the top and bottom of the shaft of the vase.

**Zaha Hadid** designed the 'Crevasse' vase for Italian firm Alessi. It is actually a set of two vases, shaped as if cut diagonally from a single block, yielding warped inverted surfaces. The two components can either be used connected, functioning as a single, solid form with two separate slots for the flowers, or they can stand apart, like two uniquely shaped skyscrapers built next to each other. The vases are available in silver, gold, bronze, gunmetal or mirror-polished steel finishes.

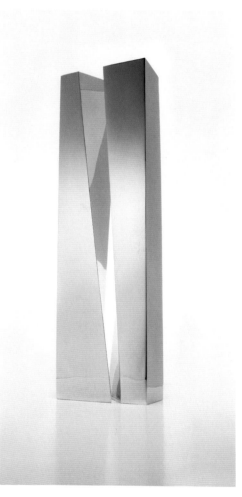

**Zaha Hadid**

The 'Fuji' vases by **Linda Bayon** of the **Traits d'Union** design team and 'Weight Vases' by **Decha Archjananun** of Bangkok-based **THINKK Studio** all play with structure, contrasting airy metal 'scaffolding' with solid, heavy bases (thick, monochrome ceramic for 'Fuji'; rough unfinished concrete for 'Weight Vases'). In both designs the lower part acts as a container to hold water and stems while the wire scaffolding allows the tops of the stems to be positioned into original floral arrangements. The separation of the two different parts of these inventive constructions, as well as the juxtaposition of completely different materials, make the vases visually interesting even without flowers.

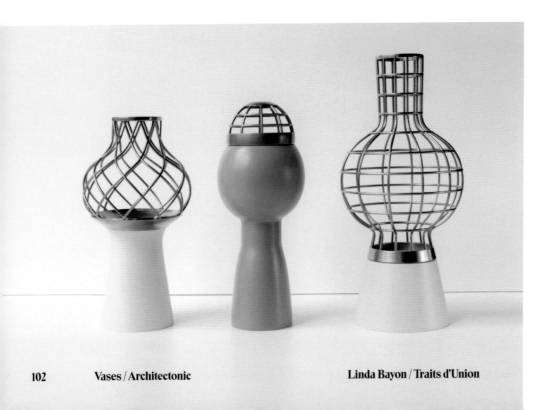

This page:
ECAL / Decha Archjananun
for THINKK Studio •
Thailand
'Weight Vases' for
Specimen Editions · 2011

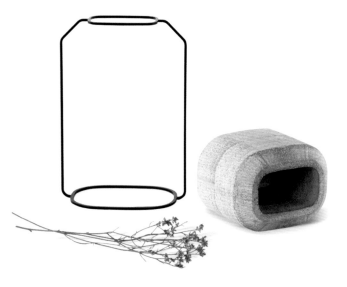

**Sebastian Herkner** gives his 'Corolle' vases a complex, sophisticated, layered architectural form that evokes flowers even without the presence of a bouquet. The coloured outer glass layer, resembling a hoop skirt, aptly refers to the idea of the petals as the dress of the flower and interacts visually with an interior structure of coloured silvered glass. 'The usual transparency becomes opaque where the pattern appears while the colors overlap and reflect on each other,' says the designer. The 'Vase Cut' collection from **AZ&MUT** duo Géraldine Hetzel and Rafaële David is another structural experiment involving two layers of coloured glass. In this case, the vase is made from a single type of glass, literally cut into two parts. The neck component can be removed to make it easier to change the water in the base container, or inverted to support shorter, wider bouquets.

This page:
**Sebastian Herkner**
• **Germany**
'Corolle' vases
for Verreum · 2016

**Opposite:**
**AZ&MUT** • **France**
'Vase Cut' collection
for Serax · 2014

**Guillaume Delvigne** has an architectural mind and his vases often resemble small, multi-component structures. Available in only 100 numbered pieces, the 'Toy' vase has hand-painted decorations, which interact with the shapes and colours of the blown glass and flat glass components to create interesting reflections and distortions. Another limited edition 'built' from multiple, contrasting components, the 'Deneb' vase is devoid of any pattern. It is a turquoise blown-glass bubble vase supported by a moulded cork tray. The two parts may be contrasting but they are also inseparable, as the glass element cannot stand on its own.

**Guillaume Delvigne • France**

**Opposite:**
'Toy' vase for
La Chance · 2015

**Below:**
'Deneb' vase for
Specimen Editions · 2010

Another vase designed by **Guillaume Delvigne** is humorously titled 'Chapeaux pour vase' ('Hats for a Vase'), consisting of a clear glass vase supplied with three different glazed porcelain 'hats' in either black or white. Again, Delvigne constructs playful towers from contrasting materials, with the heavily textured porcelain sitting atop a transparent glass base. 'VASE1' from **UAU project** has a similar construction. In this case, the product consists only of a 3D-printed bioplastic neck (made from PLA filaments, which are renewable and 100% biodegradable). To build the vase, simply position the neck on any clean, wide-mouth jar filled with water.

**Opposite and above right:**
**UAU project • Poland**
'VASE1' · 2017

**Right:**
**Guillaume Delvigne • France**
'Chapeaux pour vase'
for Industreal · 2004

**Nir Meiri** found inspiration for his 'Babilus' vases in 'the architecture of ancient cities, temples and altars'. The vases are made of a combination of natural materials such as bamboo and wood with glass or Corian, individually turned and then stacked layer by layer around a glass vessel. Displayed as a group, they evoke the skyline of an ancient city such as Babylon. Meiri's 'Florence' vases are similarly constructed by stacking contrasting materials (copper and wood) around a glass vessel, but their smooth, tubular forms have a more modern, minimalist appearance. Flowers held in the transparent glass vessel above the tray-like circular rim look as if they are being presented on a pedestal.

Nir Meiri • Israel/UK

**Below:**
'Florence' vases · 2016

**Opposite:**
'Babilus' vases · 2014

These pages:
**Studio RSW • Germany**
'Maket' collection
for Pulpo · 2017

'Maket', from **Studio RSW** for German firm Pulpo, is a visually intriguing collection of ceramic vases featuring interlocking components in varying finishes, unconventional shapes and contrasting colours. The round, stepped tops are covered in a shiny, bubbled 'fat lava' glaze, contrasting with the smooth, matt-finish bases in vibrant hues. The vases can be built in various configurations, as the tops can also function as bases and vice-versa (*see opposite*). Each playful piece is handmade and thus displays unique variation.

**Studio RSW**

This page:
**Sophie Dries • France**
'Traces' vases · 2017

Opposite:
**Apparatu • Spain**
'Arquitecturas' vase · 2012

These composite vase designs by **Sophie Dries** and **Apparatu** tease our senses with their intriguing towers of contrasting materials and textures. Dries's 'Traces' collection explores how black clay and shiny metals interact in multi-storey constructions that juxtapose rough and smooth surfaces. The 'Arquitecturas' vase from family-run ceramics studio Apparatu also features architectural layers of contrasting colours and surface textures, although in this case all components are ceramic: a shiny marbled stoneware base, a white stucco-finish body, and an unfinished terracotta collar. The three components can be dismantled and assembled in other configurations.

**Sophie Dries**

Opposite:
**Marta Bakowski • France**
'Chimney Containers'
· 2015

This page:
**Éric Jourdan • France**
'Jo' vases for Ligne Roset
· 2012

Chimney-like shapes are ideal for vases. **Marta Bakowski** experiments with softly tinted concrete to explore, as she states, 'the potential and poetics of colour within a common construction material'. Each element of her handmade 'Chimney Containers', primarily used as vases, is in a different hue. **Éric Jourdan** creates a very different chimney-like form, realized in more conventional enamelled ceramic with a gloss finish in various colours. His imaginatively shaped 'Jo' vases offer flowers a support and enhance their scent by directing it forward and upward.

Marta Bakowski

Chimney-like architectonic structures also feature in vases from **Numéro 111** and **Alnoor Design**. The 'Karlos' vase from Numéro 111 for Ligne Roset consists of a square ceramic tube on a marble base against a matte epoxy lacquered steel 'wall'. Alnoor's enamelled ceramic 'Cheminy' for Roche Bobois features two superimposed cubic elements resembling a square chimney atop a rectangular building (the name of the vase is a play on the French for chimney, *cheminée*). Flowers displayed against the wall in 'Karlos' or extending from the top element of 'Cheminy' contrast in interesting ways with both architectonic forms.

**Right:**
**Alnoor Design • France**
'Cheminy' vase for
Roche Bobois · 2017

**Opposite:**
**Numéro 111 • France**
'Karlos' vase for
Ligne Roset · 2015

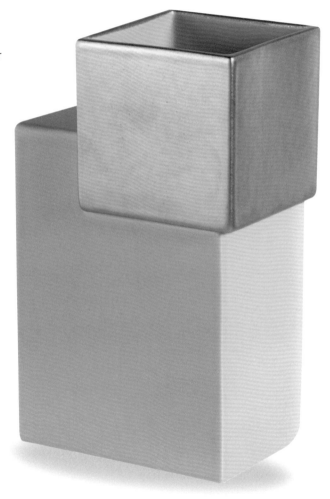

Two very different designs create flexible tower displays. **Bruce and Stéphanie Tharp** of studio Materious designed a collection of colourful vase sections for Ligne Roset in moulded enamelled ceramic: the large section holds water; the two medium sections function as risers or extension rings, and the smallest can be placed on top to display a single flower or a small spray. In 1965 **Joe Colombo** created his tower-like '2-in-1' vase that, turned upside down, could also serve as a drinking vessel. It has recently been re-released by Lyngby Porcelæn in several combinations of clear and tinted hand-blown glass.

**Left:**
**Emmanuel Babled • Portugal**
'Koori' vases for Venini
· 2016

**Opposite:**
**Aldo Bakker • Netherlands**
'Crystal Vase' collection for
Atelier Swarovski · 2016

As **Aldo Bakker** remarks, 'The beauty of crystal is that it can be both fluid and architectural.' His first collaboration with Swarovski is a series of vases combining crystal glass and polished stone (marble and pink onyx) in a faceted shape that holds a single stem in its centre and generates fascinating light effects. **Emmanuel Babled**'s 'Koori' vases for Venini fuse highly polished blown glass with another surprising 'architectural' material: cement, with a satin finish. The two strongly contrasting sections create light effects through their interplay of transparency and opacity.

Above:
Gert-Jan Soepenberg
• Netherlands
'Vase #1' · 2014

Opposite:
Lara Bohinc • Slovenia/UK
'Fortress' vases · 2016

Some designers create vases inspired by famous buildings. 'Vase #1' is the first in **Gert-Jan Soepenberg**'s series of architecture-derived vases. Fascinated by Oscar Niemeyer's Palácio da Alvorada in Brazil's capital city Brasília, Soepenberg has abstracted the characteristic element of the building to become the form of the vase. **Lara Bohinc**'s hexagonal, interlocking block structures were similarly inspired by the octagonal towers of the Diocletian Palace in Croatia. Her four different 'Fortress' vases emphasize the interplay of light and shade on their intricate, angular surfaces.

**Lara Bohinc**

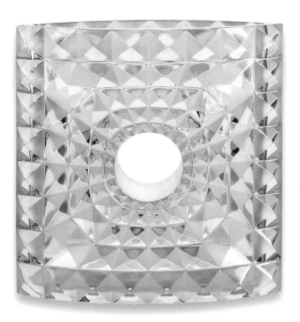

'This vase can be interpreted as the miniature of a large palace.' Mario Botta

Mario Botta • Switzerland
'Géo' vase for Lalique
· 2014

Renowned architect **Mario Botta** also makes architecture in miniature, realized in dazzling crystal. His limited-edition 'Géo' vase for Lalique takes the basic building shape of a square, patterned with three-dimensional, pyramid-like elements and a pierced circle in the centre, which combined to resemble the sun radiating light. Botta's inspiration for the geometric patterning on the vase was the diamond-carved marble exterior of the Palazzo dei Diamanti in Ferrara, Italy.

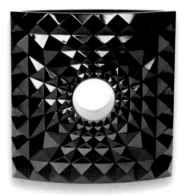

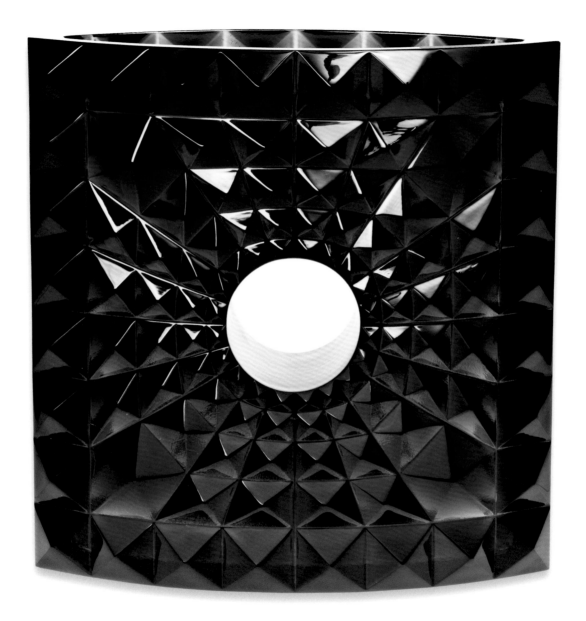

**Mario Botta**

SCULPTURAL

# Q&A with Erik Olovsson

**After designing many inventive objects, you decided to explore vases. Why?**

I had a new curiosity about glass. My girlfriend and I are also into plants and flowers and had our eyes on various planters and vases at the time. I like to make stuff for myself, developing projects from that. When I was looking at vases in general they were all very delicate and fragile. I wanted to do something different so I started to investigate whether I could combine stone and glass.

**Was a vase a challenging object to design?**

I really enjoyed the process. The more I started to think about it, the more I liked the idea of making an object designed for carrying flowers. Every design has its own challenges, but with this project the most challenging part was in the production stage, especially finding the right people to work with. It took some trial and error in finding the right stones and the right material for the glass forms. But when making the first glass pieces I was quite surprised to see that the final pieces looked almost exactly like the first paper sketches I had made one year earlier.

**What was more important for you in the creative process: function or aesthetic value?**

I like to have function or a purpose as a base for my projects and then see how far I can go from there – how far can I go but still have the function of a vase? For this project ['Indefinite Vases'] the material properties have given the pieces their forms. When making the glass pieces on top of the sharp edges, the most interesting part is how the glass floats. You can't really control every part of the production, but that is what makes every piece unique and what keeps me wanting to explore further.

**What was the inspiration for the 'Indefinite Vases' collection?**

I'm very interested in stones and think they all have an interesting story to tell. I've been researching different kinds of stone over the last few years and have been on a couple of trips to Italy to learn more about them and their production.

I'm always inspired by visiting factories to see the full spectrum of stone production. In most projects my main reason to explore and to make things is to satisfy my own curiosity.

**By pushing the boundaries of traditional materials and experimenting with forms your designs redefine a vase. You place it closer to sculpture than to other design objects. What should a contemporary vase be like?**

For me that's an interesting place to be, in between sculpture and design objects. That's where I feel you can make the most interesting pieces. In general, I like objects that make me feel something from looking at them. They should talk to me.

**Right:**
**Erik Olovsson • Sweden**
'Indefinite Vases' · 2016

**Preceding pages:**
**Zaha Hadid and**
**Gareth Neal • UK**
'Ves-el' vases · 2014

**Cédric Ragot** experimented with the plasticity of porcelain to see how far he could go in (de) forming shapes. Solid yet dynamic, his sculptural designs were often inspired by nature, such as the structure of rocks in 'Geode' or a whirlwind in 'Squall' (both designed for Rosenthal). The limited-edition 'Palm' vase was created through a process called slip casting (liquid clay is poured into moulds to form a layer on its inside walls). Its harmonious curtain-like form is a visual delight.

Cédric Ragot • France

**Above:**
'Geode' vase for Rosenthal · 2015/2016

**Left:**
'Squall' vase for Rosenthal · 2015/2016

This page:
**Cédric Ragot • France**
'Palm' vases for Bitossi
Ceramiche · 2013

In pursuit of unique and atypical shapes, fashion designer **Stine Goya** reinterprets historical ceramic techniques in the very contemporary silhouette of her 'Fiora' vase. The vase's peculiar yet strikingly precise form is emphasized by its shiny monochrome outer surface, which creates fascinating reflections. World-renowned architect Frank Gehry designed a series of vases for Tiffany & Co. The asymmetrical form of his bone china 'Rock' vase takes centre stage, with a monochrome white finish similarly drawing attention to its sculptural precision.

**Stine Goya • Denmark**
'Fiora' vase for Kähler
Design · 2016

Artist **David Wiseman** creates 'poetic and sculptural work spanning the spectrum of fine and decorative arts'. The irregular shapes of his vases evoke natural phenomena and have expressive sculptural presence. Wiseman often plays with textures. Whether he selects stainless steel, as in his 'Polished Rock' vase, or bronze, as in 'Scoria', the designer focuses precisely on the qualities of each material and allows them to inspire the three-dimensional form and surface textures of his sculptural vessels.

**David Wiseman • USA**

**Above:**
'Scoria' vase · 2011–14

**Opposite:**
'Polished Rock' vase · 2011

Glass artist **Jeff Zimmerman**'s signature crumpled sculptural vessels in mirrored, hand-blown glass take sensational shapes that speak to the imagination. The form of each vase is unique. The artist is also known for his experimental sculptures. While drawing on traditional glassblowing techniques, his visual language is contemporary. The plasticity of the material inspires the dramatic shapes he achieves by pushing, pulling, dripping and spinning. These fantastical vases are actually art pieces, which demand equally unconventional flower arrangements. 'Disturbing beauty', as the artist calls it, is the main goal.

**Jeff Zimmerman • USA**

**Above:**
Unique crumpled sculptural vessel in silver mirrored hand-blown glass with white top · 2016

**Right:**
Unique crumpled sculptural vessel in orange mirrored hand-blown glass with white murrine · 2015

**Opposite:**
Unique crumpled sculptural vessel in silver mirrored hand-blown glass with celadon top and applied glass gems · 2015

Jeff Zimmerman

The 'Blown Shapes' collection by **Bold** is a celebration of the art of glass-blowing, pushing the limits of the technology. The abstract, organic sculptural shapes of the 40 unique vases are accentuated by an interesting palette of colours. Inspired by the skilful gesture of the craftsman, the collection is also an excellent example of how traditional techniques can produce very contemporary forms. These dramatic, imposing sculptural pieces can be, but don't have to be, complemented by flowers.

**Bold • France**
'Blown Shapes' vases
· 2010

**'Look at a glass-blower, and you will see, in the power of fire mixed with the finesse of glass, the high sophistication of his work.'** Bold

**Arik Levy** and **Nicolas Triboulot** also experiment with unexpected sculptural shapes in glass, in this case inspired by crystal's complex structure and ability to play with light. Levy's 'Crystal Rock' vase is 'a perfectly cut, yet roughly sculpted contemporary silex that highlights the interaction between light and darkness'. Triboulot's 'Diva' vase has an innovative reclining silhouette and a folded sculptural form that employs the magic of reflection. The reclining shape not only serves as a sculptural centrepiece on its own, but also allows a large bouquet to decorate a table without blocking the view of people sitting opposite it.

Poetic and visually surprising, 'Indefinite Vases' by **Erik Olovsson** are made of colourful marble and hand-blown glass. The sculptural designs play with oppositions of solidity and fragility and explore the relationship between geometric and organic forms by literally fusing them together. Melting and softly curved glass rests on sturdy, irregularly formed stone bases. While these are functional vases, they are also sculptural objects, making complex statements in their own right.

**These pages:**
**Erik Olovsson • Sweden**
'Indefinite Vases' · 2016

Industrial designer **Falke Svatun** has created a vase with a cleverly sculpted cutout at the base that allows it to merge with the edge of a table, windowsill or shelf, challenging the conventional approach to vase shape, function and appearance. The cutout is, however, shallow enough to allow the stoneware 'Tumble' vase to rest on a flat surface, seemingly defying gravity, like a free-standing abstract sculpture.

While elegant marble is the classic material for a monumental sculpture, it can also be worked with astonishing lightness to create beautiful, airy vases. **Lorenzo Damiani**'s Carrara marble vase from the 'Boboli' collection for Pusterla Marmi is built of tiny, carefully sculpted elements resembling broken eggshells, joined only where their edges touch so that they appear to float in midair. Carrara-born designers **Moreno Ratti** and **Paolo Ulian** collaborated on 'Little Gerla', a limited-edition collection of four vases, each made from a single piece of recycled marble tile cut with a water jet into concentric rings which are then stacked, rotated and glued together. Their intricate ribbon-like shapes deceive the eye and bring a sense of lightness to the solid object.

**This page:**
**Moreno Ratti and Paolo Ulian • Italy**
'Little Gerla' vases · 2015

**Opposite:**
**Lorenzo Damiani • Italy**
'Boboli' vase for
Pusterla Marmi · 2016

These colourful, fantastical structures take us into the amazing world of artist **Thaddeus Wolfe**'s glass sculptures. Inspired by artistic movements of the 20th century, particularly Cubism and Art Deco, as well as by Czech Cubist architecture, Wolfe creates unique vases and vessels from hand-blown, moulded, cut and polished glass. Their contrasting surfaces (some polished, others jagged, bubbled or rough), sharp edges, remarkable patterns and abstract forms surprise and intrigue the viewer. Wolfe makes his own moulds and has invented a unique fabrication process to push the limits of the glass in order to obtain his phenomenal angular forms.

**Thaddeus Wolfe • USA**

**Above:**
'Unique Assemblage Vessel in Handblown, Cut and Polished Glass' · 2015

**Right:**
'Unique Assemblage Vessel in Handblown, Cut and Polished Glass' · 2015

**Opposite:**
'Unique Assemblage Vessel in Handblown, Cut and Polished Glass' · 2014

**Thaddeus Wolfe**

**Thaddeus Wolfe**

**Right:**
Leonardo Talarico • Italy
'Stems' vases for
Cappellini · 2016

**Below:**
Jean-François D'Or
• Belgium
'Cutting' vase
for Ligne Roset · 2008

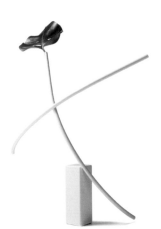

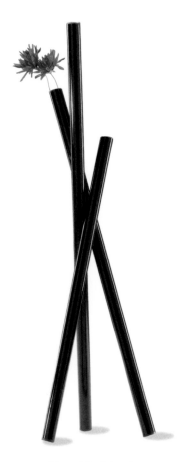

The 'Stems' vase designed by **Leonardo Talarico** resembles one of Alexander Calder's sculptural mobiles. Two slender 'stem'-like tubes are not only poetically intertwined, but also cleverly suspended in the air. Although the stems are fixed discretely to a cubic base, they appear to be in motion when holding single flowers, as the perspective changes so quickly depending on the viewing angle. **Jean-François D'Or**'s branch-like 'Cutting' vase, however, is actually mobile, as the joints holding together the three tall steel tubes (150, 130 and 110 cm) can be adjusted to allow a variety of positions. Each tube contains a borosilicate glass element to hold the flowers.

Two other sculptural tube designs push the boundaries even further. A.C.V Studio's **Anna Varendorff** makes limited-edition and handmade vases from fragile brass tubes soldered to a base plate and bent in unusual configurations that enable truly unique flower arrangements, although due to their fragility the tubes can hold only delicate stems. The 'Solo' vase by **Guilherme Wentz** also explores the tubular shape. His 1-metre tall vases are not designed to be free-standing, however, and must be mounted against a wall. The designer says that both the shape of the tube and the cutting technique used to create the curve detail are inspired by cane and bamboo work.

Left:
**Guilherme Wentz • Brazil**
'Solo' vase · 2017

Below:
**Anna Varendorff • Australia**
'Edging Over' vase (left);
'Uneven U' vase (centre);
and 'Double Circle U' vase
(right) all for A.C.V Studio
· 2015

**Anna Varendorff / Guilherme Wentz**

These vases are inspired by the construction of clothes and play with the idea of a shape in space – **Sebastian Herkner** with an actual three-dimensional element, and **Emmanuel Babled** by applying a refined pattern. Herkner's 'Falda' is a conventionally shaped bulbous vase surmounted by a pleated high collar, which helps to support the flowers. Its shiny golden titanium inner coating contrasts with the velvety outer surface of the biscuit porcelain. Babled's 'Kimono' vase also features a striking inner layer, in this case brightly coloured blown glass, contrasting with a white outer surface, here made of a combination of opaline white and transparent glass. The bands of transparent glass on the exterior mimic a tied kimono sash and accentuate the vase's three-dimensional shape.

**Right:**
**Emmanuel Babled • Portugal**
'Kimono' vase for Venini
· 2013

**Opposite:**
**Sebastian Herkner**
**• Germany**
'Falda' vase
for Rosenthal · 2014

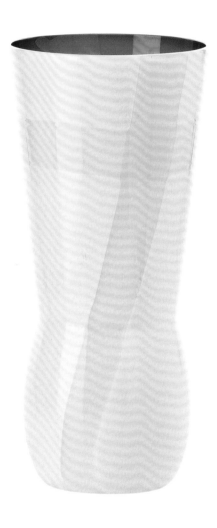

Left:
**Paolo Dell'Elce • Italy**
'Via Fondazza' vases
for Skultuna · 2014

A slender, perfectly sculpted bottle-shaped vase is ideal for a single stem. **Paolo Dell'Elce** draws inspiration from Giorgio Morandi's minimalist still-life paintings. 'Via Fondazza' (named for the artist's address in Bologna) is a range of seamless vases, resembling elegant bottles, in polished spun brass manufactured by Swedish company Skultuna. Another Swedish manufacturer, known for being the oldest operating glassworks in the country, collaborated with **Kjell Engman** to create an extraordinarily colourful series of bottle-vases. The 'Fidji' vases incorporate rainbow effects that accentuate the flowers' hues. The 'Sorori' vase from **Nousaku** is made of brass (in four different finishes) using traditional casting techniques. Its form is inspired by the single-stem flower vase that is a traditional component of a Japanese tea ceremony.

**Paolo Dell'Elce**

**Above:**
**Nousaku • Japan**
'Sorori' vase · 2002

**Right:**
**Kjell Engman • Sweden**
'Fidji' vase for Kosta Boda
· undated

**Nousaku / Kjell Engman**

'We can't fully control the design, but we also let
it be random. It's important for us to be connected
to the vases. We need to be the ones who make
the final pattern on the shape.' Studio Oddness

Studio Oddness (Adrianus Kundert and Thomas van der Sman) and **Marie Liebhardt** experiment with textures and finishes to give the surfaces of their vases a three-dimensional appearance. Kundert and van der Sman developed a special technique for their 'Bubblegraphy' collection, which involves applying a soap layer on the surface when the ceramic vases are shaped. 'Air is then blown into the glaze, creating an extraordinary pattern of playful bubbles', explain the designers. The uniquely textured skin of Liebhardt's 'Flaws' vases, made via a process of pouring thin layers of coloured porcelain into a plaster mould, resembles aging, weathered walls with peeling layers.

**Marie Liebhardt**

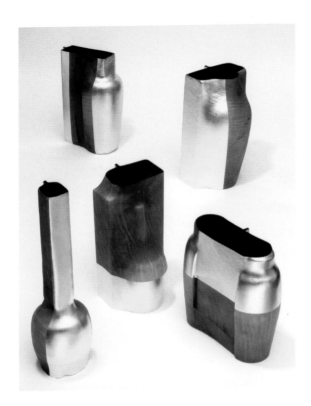

These vases are sculpted from traditional materials using innovative techniques. **Simon Hasan** combines boiled leather with polyurethane resin and 22-carat gold or palladium gilding, using the medieval process of *cuir bouili* to obtain his vases' unusual shapes, which are based on the forms of antique wine bottles. **Zaha Hadid**'s limited-edition white oak 'Ves-el' vases were designed in collaboration with **Gareth Neal** for an exhibition at the Victoria and Albert Museum during the London Design Festival. The idea was to explore traditional craft techniques such as hand-thrown pottery, raised silverware and fluted carving through digital fabrication and mechanical processes. They began with a traditional vessel form and distorted it digitally, producing a striking final shape with an extended open slit at one end.

**Above:**
**Simon Hasan • UK**
'Vase Family: 2nd Generation' · 2009

**Opposite:**
**Zaha Hadid and Gareth Neal • UK**
'Ves-el' vases · 2014

'Using the traditional vessel form as a starting point and subverting its appearance to dramatic extremes, the design embodies a sense of the handmade through the arm of a robot, questioning the viewer's perception of craft and the handmade.' Gareth Neal

**Zaha Hadid and Gareth Neal**

These sculptural vases, both made from materials used in building construction, appear almost two-dimensional in shape. **Jiwon Choi**'s 'Tyvek' vase is made from a lightweight and tear-resistant material produced from plastic fibres and more typically used as a moisture barrier in house-building. Choi made her prototype as packaging for a bunch of flowers. In contrast, **Kateryna Sokolova**'s 'Mold' vase is realized in rough, heavy unfinished concrete, with a hidden glass tube to hold the flowers. The vase's form, too, is intentionally unfinished, retaining the untrimmed 'wings' of products created in construction moulding.

**Jiwon Choi** •
**South Korea/USA**
'Tyvek' vases · 2013

**Kateryna Sokolova**
• **Ukraine**
'Mold' vases for
Ligne Roset · 2015

**Kateryna Sokolova**

Clean, abstract, minimalist forms exert dramatic
sculptural presence, as in the 'Volcapeli'
collection from experimental ceramics studio
**Atelier Polyhedre** (founded by Baptiste Ymonet
and Vincent Jousseaume). The geometric yet
zoomorphic forms of the stoneware pitchers
(which the designers say can also be used as
vases) evoke volcanoes and the shape of a
pelican's beak, and each is named for its basic
shape ('Triangle', 'Rectangle' and 'Trapèze'). They
make an intriguing display as a group, as do the
massive, sculptural shapes of the four terracotta
(with grey engobe) 'Dome' vases designed by
architect **Kristina Dam**.

Atelier Polyhedre • France
'Volcapeli' collection · 2016

**Kristina Dam • Denmark**
'Dome' vases · 2016

These ceramic vases from **Antonio Forteleoni** and **THINKK Studio** take inspiration from the sculptural forms of ancient handmade vessels. Forteleoni's 'Jana' is a collection of vases made from a black clay typical of Sardinia, with a rough exterior reminiscent of wheel-thrown pottery. Its form is a contemporary reinterpretation of the shape of ancient storage vessels. Ancient pottery was also the source of inspiration for THINKK's 'Epoch' series, which was realized by using a handmade prototype and contemporary mould-casting techniques.

These vases were literally shaped by the lives of their makers. Swedish studio **Front Design** teamed up with the Siyazama Project, a collective of women working with traditional beadcraft in KwaZulu-Natal, South Africa. The prototypes of the designs were created during a workshop in Durban in 2010. 'The Story Vases tell the personal stories of five women from South Africa', explains the studio. 'They told about their daily lives, their husbands and children. They shared their hopes and dreams, and talked about love, life and death. Their stories also touch on such serious subjects as the effect of HIV on their society, poverty and unemployment. They talked about their business and what beadwork meant to them.' Parts of these stories were applied to the vases by threading glass beads onto metal wires, which were later made into vase-shaped moulds used to blow the glass.

**Front Design • Sweden**
**Siyazama Project**
**• South Africa**
'Story Vases' for
Editions in Craft · 2011

**Front Design and Siyazama Project**

Yukihiro Kaneuchi and Aurelie Tu look to
the world of fabrics for sculptural form and
textural nuances. Kaneuchi's porcelain vase for
Secondome takes the shape of a classic vase
tightly bound with red ribbon, which visually
transforms the bouquet it holds into an elegantly
wrapped gift. The 'Asira' decorative vases
designed by Aurelie Tu for Ligne Roset are made
from woollen felt that has been cut and woven by
hand. The bi-coloured material allows the surface
to be covered with complex ornamental patterns.
Tu's vases can be used for dried arrangements
or as decorative covers for a jar or glass of
water holding fresh flowers.

**Yukihiro Kaneuchi • Japan**
'Ribbon' vase for
Secondome and Fabrica
· 2009

Yukihiro Kaneuchi

**Olivier van Herpt**'s ceramic vessels inspired by the 2017 Spring/Summer collection of clothing brand COS were sculpted in a natural material (clay) using cutting-edge technology. His pioneering 3D-printing and digital fabrication methods use clay to create a set of six exceptional vases whose shapes, colours and textures evoke the fabrics used for the COS collection. 'It's almost as if the clothing and wearer merge together to create new forms, and I used this idea as the starting point to develop the vases', explains the designer. The vases are textured in tiny ridges that are visible when they are seen up close.

This minimalist design by **Enzo Mari** for the traditional manufacturer Königliche Porzellan-Manufaktur Berlin has a poetic sculptural presence. The porcelain vase rises elegantly, in a wing-like shape, from a tiny slab of brushed stainless steel that serves as a base. The original vase was white, but it is now produced in a number of colourful painted patterns.

**Right:**
**Enzo Mari • Italy**
'Mari' vase for Königliche
Porzellan-Manufaktur
Berlin · 1994

**Opposite:**
**Olivier van Herpt**
**• Netherlands**
'COS × Olivier van Herpt'
vases for COS · 2017

**Enzo Mari**

WITH A TWIST

# Q&A with Front Design
## — Sofia Lagerkvist and Anna Lindgren

**Quite a few of your projects are vases. Why do you find them so interesting to design?**

Throughout time and in different cultures the vase has had a similar shape. This shape is something almost everyone can recognize and refer to. The vase can be an everyday object or a valuable art piece. A simple terracotta vessel or a richly decorated porcelain vase can have the same shape. Because vases can be made out of so many different materials, such as ceramics, glass, wood and metal, you work with very few limitations.

**Thinking of designs with a twist, your creations are the first thing that spring to mind. How do you come up with ideas for your amazing vases?**

We develop the ideas as a team. Each of us has a different input, searching for the best idea and refining it before we start to sketch and build models. Together we create things that no one could have achieved alone. It is, of course, more fun to work together.

**You challenge us by playing with the most common and traditional vase forms and materials. How does this approach benefit your vase designs?**

We want all our pieces to have a direct aesthetic expression, but often they also have a story to tell about the process, the material or the context in which the product was made. We are interested in objects and how they describe their own times. It is interesting to observe everyday items that you usually do not notice. Our 'Design by Surrounding' vase, for example, plays with this question. The reflection of the room it has been standing in becomes the permanent decoration of the vase and mixes with the new reflection, like a double-exposed image. If you can look at the things you already have in your home, and see something new, then we have succeeded.

**A contemporary vase should be...?**

Perhaps the vase should be biodegradable, and able to follow the different life stages of the flowers it holds.

Above:
**Front Design • Sweden**
'Blow Away Vase'
for Moooi · 2009

Preceding pages:
**Robin van Hontem**
**• Netherlands**
'Dancing Vases' · 2009

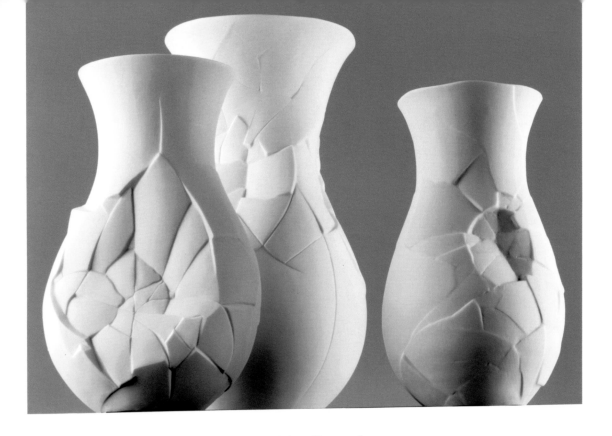

'I began by busting a lot of vases. After discovering the time-consuming effort of putting the pieces back together, I lined the interior of one with silicone rubber to keep the pieces in place upon impact. I then dipped the vessel into liquid porcelain to fill in the cracks.' Dror Benshetrit

Vases / With a Twist                    **Dror Benshetrit**

Vases can be as fragile as the flowers they hold and are usually made of easily breakable materials. In an eccentric innovation, **Dror Benshetrit** makes breakage the vase's defining decorative feature. His cracked and shattered porcelain 'Vase of Phases' collection for Rosenthal appears to have been smashed and then glued clumsily back together. **Jakub Berdych**'s 'Born Broken' is inspired by errors in the glassblowing process. 'Each blown shape is broken into several segments to create a pattern visually akin to cutting', explains manufacturer Lasvit. The elements are then reheated together to form a single, watertight vessel with bands of intriguing chips and cracks.

**Right:**
**Jakub Berdych**
• **Czech Republic**
'Born Broken' vases
for Lasvit · 2016

**Opposite:**
**Dror Benshetrit • Israel/USA**
'Vase of Phases' collection
for Rosenthal · 2005

**Jakub Berdych**

**Vases / With a Twist**

**Itamar Burstein** and **Hans Tan** also play with breakage in deconstructing the classic vase silhouette. The broken asymmetrical lines of Burstein's enamelled faience 'Daphna' vase create an intriguing play of light and shadow, as also in his 'Polygon Silhouette', where the complex asymmetrical structure suggests broken pieces that have been incorrectly reassembled. Tan fills a hand-blown borosilicate glass shell with porcelain shards from a reclaimed toilet bowl, as if to show the dual character of porcelain, which can be both decorative and very utilitarian. 'This is not a porcelain vase, but a vase (-like) porcelain', says the designer.

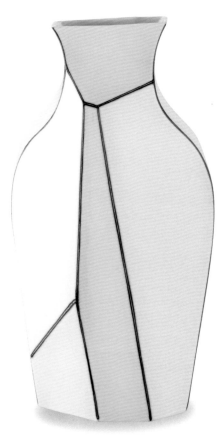

Itamar Burstein • Israel

**Above:**
'Polygon Silhouette' vase for Ligne Roset · 2017

**Left:**
'Daphna' vase for Ligne Roset · 2017

These pages:
**Yiannis Ghikas • Greece**
'Mutant Vase' · 2014

**Yiannis Ghikas** has created a 3D-printed vase inspired by the special effects in science fiction movies that show alien creatures moving under a person's skin. The impression of something pushing through to the surface from the inside is expressed by the gradual transition from perfectly smooth to ribbed outer surface, visible when the vase is rotated or walked around. The designer describes the vase as having 'a "mutation" that gradually appears and disappears'.

A puff of wind can topple a house of cards, but it should not be powerful enough to blow away porcelain. **Front Design** and **Cédric Ragot** have created vase designs that appear to be distorted by the wind. Front's 'Blow Away Vase' for Moooi was created by digitizing a Royal Delft vase, adding new parameters to the material using 3D software, and then exposing it to a simulated gust of wind. Ragot's already iconic 'Hyper Fast' vase similarly distorts the classical vase form in porcelain. The design was originally made in a limited edition for French firm YMER&MALTA, and a larger collection based on this concept was later mass-produced by Rosenthal.

**Front Design • Sweden**
'Blow Away Vase'
for Moooi · 2009

**Cédric Ragot • France**
'Hyper Fast' vase for
YMER&MALTA · 2003

**Cédric Ragot**

Master artisan Joan Mañosa of family-run studio **Apparatu** hand-turned a limited edition of three hundred intentionally flawed ceramic vases. 'The process needed to be wrong', reads the project statement. 'Accidents were welcome.' The vases, each one unique and distinguished by a different kind of mistake, are deliberately imperfect and thus celebrate hand craftsmanship. The ceramic appears fluid and in motion, and some pieces seemingly resemble the texture of fabric, creating interesting light effects. Twisted, stretched and contorted, the '300' collection is as eccentric as it is captivating.

**Fulvio Bianconi • Italy**
'Fazzoletto Bicolore' vases
for Venini · 1948/2016

In his 'Fazzoletto Bicolore' vase, legendary
Italian designer and glassmaker Fulvio Bianconi
emphasized the plasticity of Murano glass. Using
the 15th-century opal technique meant to imitate
porcelain, Bianconi obtained a cellophane-like
effect in this striking vase with its surprising,
playful shape resembling an opened candy
wrapper. The bold, vivid colours – marine blue
on the outer surface and red inside – skilfully
highlight the folded edges.

François Azambourg and Robin van Hontem have invented another twist: vases that defy gravity. Azambourg created ceramic vases composed of three different units (in colour combinations of white, black, yellow and green) that resemble upside-down bowling pins in shape. Despite being very narrow at the bottom and larger at the top, the vases are deceptively stable. Van Hontem based his series of nylon and ceramic vases on a spinning top in motion. Typically, a top spins quickly, then wobbles as it slows and finally tips over. The designer's vases seemingly freeze the 'top' in various positions while it is wobbling or 'dancing' – hence 'Dancing Vases'.

**Left:**
**François Azambourg**
• **France**
'3 Vases' for
Cappellini · 2008

**Opposite:**
**Robin van Hontem**
• **Netherlands**
'Dancing Vases' · 2009

François Azambourg

**Robin van Hontem**

This page:
**Thomas Wenzel • Germany**
'Bulb' vases for Königlische
Porzellan-Manufaktur
Berlin · 2016

**Opposite:**
**Hallgeir Homstvedt**
**• Norway**
'Balance Vase'
set for Muuto · 2014

The concept of balance inspired these unconventional vases by **Thomas Wenzel** and **Hallgeir Homstvedt**. Wenzel's 'Bulb' for Königlische Porzellan-Manufaktur Berlin is modelled on the shape of laboratory beakers, but with a playful tilt, as if slightly off balance. The bicoloured porcelain brings beautiful visual effects to the minimalist design. The 'Balance Vase' set designed by Homstvedt for Muuto seemingly defies gravity. It consists of three clay vases in different shapes and shades fixed to a steel tray by magnets hidden in their bases. The magnets are strong enough to keep the vases upright, but also allow them to be moved around on the tray.

**Hallgeir Homstvedt**

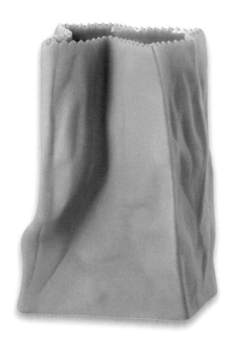

The playful element in these **Tapio Wirkkala** and **Hella Jongerius** designs lies in their deceptive use of materials. Wirkkala's iconic vase appears to be a paper bag that has been slightly smashed. In reality it is made of porcelain, perfectly stable and capable of being filled with water. The opposite concept is embodied in Jongerius's vase, which looks like a typical glass or ceramic vase, but is actually made from extremely flexible polyurethane rubber that allows the vase to be folded for storage. 'The perception of an existing, archetypal vase is changed', says Jongerius, 'due to the application of a soft material where our collective memory expects a hard material'. Filled with water, however, it is just as suitable for flowers as a regular vase.

**Hella Jongerius**
**• Netherlands**
'Soft Vase' for
Droog Design · 1994

These pages:
**Scholten & Baijings**
**• Netherlands**
'Paper Porcelain'
vases for HAY · 2015

The design of the 'Paper Porcelain' vase by **Scholten & Baijings** is playfully inspired by the texture of paper – in this case, coarse recycled paper. The special ceramic used for the vase even includes some iron specks to mimic the paper's surface texture as closely as possible. The form, which resembles regularly folded angular cardboard, was actually made from a hand-crafted paper model, which the designers prefer to computer modelling programs.

**Scholten & Baijings**

**Pepe Heykoop** uses an unusual vase material – leather – to create unexpected shapes. The soft leather outer skin of his 'Phased Vases' appears to be collapsing or wilting, but is actually supported by a hard plastic resin inner layer that allows the vessel to hold water. According to the designer, the slumping forms 'follow blooming flowers in a vase through their withering process'. His 'Snail Vases', another leather series (waterproofed with pine resin and beeswax), have an adaptable shape that lets them be mounted on discarded objects, such as a desk stapler or old teapot, which they appear to 'climb' like garden snails.

**Pepe Heykoop • Netherlands**

**Right:**
'Snail Vases' · 2014

**Opposite:**
'Phased Vases' · 2015

**Pepe Heykoop**

'I was fascinated by ikebana as traditional Japanese floral arrangement. Ikebana often emphasizes other areas of the plant, such as its stems and leaves, and ... shape, line and form. I believe in the spiritual aspects of ikebana and flowers in general.'

Omer Polak

**Omer Polak**'s series of ikebana vases (whose formal names, 'Vase No. 165/114/21', denote the number of flowers that can fit in each vase model) incorporate innovative pierced round metal frames for creating flexible, interesting flower arrangements over a narrow, shallow stone water-trough. Inspired by aesthetics of ikebana, the ancient Japanese tradition of flower arranging, the vases allow the flower stems to become as much the visual decorative focus as the flower-heads.

Omer Polak • Israel

**Above and opposite:**
'Vase No. 114' · 2016

**Left:**
'Vase No. 165' · 2016

This page:
**Krafla • Poland/Netherlands**
'Fly's Eye Vase' · 2015

The intriguing shape of this ikebana-style vase was inspired by visionary American architect R. Buckminster Fuller's Fly's Eye Dome, a prototype portable home. Designed by **Krafla**, the vase is constructed of two elements: a barely visible water container, over which sits a tall perforated dome. Each hole in the dome holds a single stem, and the regular position of the holes automatically arranges the flowers in a perfectly balanced display.

A wall-hung flower vase? A living still-life with flowers? American design and manufacturing collaborative **Kókili Projects** makes this extravagant idea happen. 'Mary's Vase', which holds fresh flowers in a glass tube suspended inside a round picture frame, available in several different hardwoods, is a twist on the idea of a still-life painting. 'Our design emerged from a consideration of "framing", creating an empty shape that delicately frames each flower', explain the designers.

This page:
**Kókili Projects • USA**
'Mary's Vase' · 2017

These vases not only display flowers, but protect and preserve them, emphasizing their fragility and preciousness. The curious shapes of **Cédric Ragot**'s 'Specimen' vases are inspired by the aesthetics of laboratory tools. Water can be poured into the vase either through the wide mouth of the protective glass vessel or into the open glass tube at the base, which carefully balances the water level. **Ronan and Erwan Bouroullec** made their 'Honda' vase from painted fibreglass with a dark hemispherical shape that holds the flowers in a protective shell-like hood. A lead weight in the rounded base holds the container upright.

**Above:**
**Cédric Ragot • France**
'SPECIMEN N°1-2, TUBA'
vase for En Verre Et Contre
Tout · 2010

**Right:**
**Ronan and Erwan Bouroullec**
**• France**
'Honda' vase for Kreo
Gallery · 2001

**Right:**
**AZ&MUT • France**
'Kodama' vases for Coming
B / 'Juliette' vases for Hartô
· 2015

The 'Kodama' vases, designed by Rafaëlle David of **AZ&MUT**, function as tall protective tubes for flowers, but have a surprising oval vertical opening that can reveal the stems of taller flowers and allow others to protrude at an angle. The name of the vase means 'wood spirit' in Japanese. Made from white clay, this vase delights with its simple yet inventive design and is available in three different sizes.

**AZ&MUT**

**Studio Wieki Somers**
**• Netherlands**
'Water Levels' vase
for Thomas Eyck · 2016

Multiple containers draw attention to the role of the vase as a vessel for holding water. 'Water Levels' from **Studio Wieki Somers** is a limited-edition vase referencing climate change by evoking increasing and decreasing volumes of water. Each chamber of the multilayered glass structure can be filled to a different water level for innovative flower arrangements. The mirrored base intensifies the visual effect of multiplicity. A simpler idea for dividing a glass vase into compartments is 'Vase Solar' designed by **Renaud Thiry**. The central core is slim and tall, and is set inside a shorter, wider vessel. Again, the two compartments can be filled to different levels or left empty to facilitate single- or multi-tiered arrangements.

**Renaud Thiry • France**
'Vase Solar' for
Roche Bobois · 2015

**Renaud Thiry**

Paweł Grobelny • Poland

**Far left and below left:**
'Recto-Verso Glass #1'
vase for CIAV Meisenthal
France · 2014

**Left and below right:**
'Recto-Verso Glass #2'
vase for CIAV Meisenthal
France · 2014

Intrigued by the idea of multiplying the uses for a vase, **Paweł Grobelny** invented ingenious reversible forms. Two different models of his blown-glass 'Recto-Verso' vases were manufactured by the famous French glassworks Meisenthal (in collaboration with Belgian glassblower Christophe Genard). One model is made from amber-coloured glass and has a textured outer surface; if you turn it upside down it becomes a bowl or a dish for small blossoms. Another vase, taller and made from plain transparent glass, can serve as a candlestick when inverted.

Left:
**Christian Ghion • France**
'Upside-Down' vase for
Ligne Roset · 2013

Below:
**Ontwerpduo • Netherlands**
'Bell-Jar' vase · 2015

The 'Upside-Down' vase from **Christian Ghion** explores a similar concept of reversibility, but only to give the vase itself a flexible form. The sensual shape can be stood either on the flat, wide base or on the narrower, asymmetrically cut neck. Flowers can be displayed in either orientation. As the vases are mouth-blown, each one is unique. The 'Bell-Jar' vase from **Ontwerpduo** has a similar form, but is not reversible. Made from a single piece of glass standing on a wooden base, the vase has a bell-jar within the vessel where small items can be displayed to complement the bouquet.

Twinning vases and reversing their forms not only gives a playful look, but also doubles the options for inventive floral arrangements. These 'Alfredo' vases by **Alfredo Häberli** and the 'Twin' vase by **Vanessa Mitrani** are executed in blown glass, with strong single colours that emphasize their unconventional shapes. While Häberli's vases (non-reversible mirror images of each other in form) are sold separately, Mitrani joins two vessels with a leather link.

**Above:**
**Vanessa Mitrani • France**
'Twin' vase for
Roche Bobois · 2016

**Left:**
**Alfredo Häberli • Argentina/ Switzerland**
'Alfredo' vases for Georg Jensen · 2015

Mattias Stenberg • Sweden

**Right:**
'Duo' vase · 2017

**Below:**
'Septum' vases · 2016
both for Kosta Boda

'*Septum* in itself means a *separating wall*, such as the partition wall between the right and left atrium and chamber in our heart,' explains **Mattias Stenberg** of his 'Septum' collection. The lower chambers of the three differently shaped vases are empty and made from coloured glass; flowers can be displayed in the clear upper section. The borderline between them gives the optical illusion of moving liquid. The colours used in the collection are inspired by Nordic glass art of the 1960s and 70s. His 'Duo' vase explores the same concept of the two-chambered vessel, vertically rather than horizontally. While one side is made of transparent glass, the other is dark brown, camouflaging the stems.

This page:
**Cristina Celestino • Italy**
'Olfattorio' vases
for Attico Design · 2015

Vases not only display and protect flowers, but can also enhance their scent, as in these innovative yet traditionally informed creations from **Cristina Celestino** and **Giuseppe Bessero Belti**. Celestino's 'Olfattorio' takes inspiration from the glass vessels used by ancient perfumers to distill floral essences. The stems and water are held in textured, cylindrical matt-finish glass bases, which support transparent bubbles that cover the flowerheads and funnel their scent through a tube opening at the top or side. Bessero reinterprets another obsolete traditional vessel, the paraffin lamp, substituting flower for flame and water for fuel. A biscuit porcelain base container and ring support a glass shade taken from an old paraffin lamp, which collects and intensifies the scent by funnelling it upwards through the 'chimney' opening.

**Cristina Celestino**

This page:
**Giuseppe Bessero Belti**
• **Italy/Germany**
'Experimenta' vases · 2015

**Benjamin Graindorge**
• **France**
'ikebanaMedulla' vase
for YMER&MALTA · 2010

One of **Benjamin Graindorge**'s goals in designing
'ikebanaMedulla' was to create a vase that would
remain 'inhabited' even without flowers. Empty,
the vase works as a stand-alone sculpture,
consisting of a slim, frame-like 'basket' made of
white or black lacquered polymer, filled with a
wild and intricate 3D-printed ABS plastic tangle
that is at once animal, vegetal and mechanical in
form. Flowers placed in the vase are supported
by the tangle and appear to climb it like jungle
vines. 'Recently I've been very attracted to this
idea of natural savagery', Graindorge adds.

**Charlie Guda** uses transparent test tubes as vases and combines them with magnifying lenses to focus on a single stem or flower. His curious structures honour 17th-century French engineer Augustin-Jean Fresnel, who created a thinner and lighter magnifying lens for use in lighthouses. Later used in car headlights, overhead projectors and ordinary magnifying glasses, the Fresnel lens is revived by Guda to enlarge and enhance every detail of a small blossom, creating surprising, larger-than-life displays.

This page:
**Charlie Guda •**
**Netherlands**
'Big Bloom' vase for
The Cottage Industry
· 2009–12

Another inventive idea for supporting the stems of flowers is offered in 'Hidden Vases' designed by **Chris Kabel** and 'Stem' vases from studio **Dubokk**. Kabel developed his project in collaboration with Spanish magazine *The Plant*. His aim was to make the vase 'disappear'. The flowers are supported by a wire frame with their stems resting in a low plate-like ceramic base filled with water, which is replenished by the glass bottle in the centre, much like a chicken waterer. There are three different models available. Dubokk's 'Stem' also uses a metal frame to support the stem, revealing its beauty. The minimalistic design has a more industrial or laboratory-like look, limited to a tiny glass vessel on a base and a metal bar with a loop to hold the stem upright.

**Right:**
**Dubokk • Denmark**
'Stem' vase for Menu · 2015

**Opposite:**
**Chris Kabel • Netherlands**
'Hidden Vases' · 2011–16

A vase without a vase: **Lambert Rainville**'s ingenious ultralight 'crown' allows stems to be placed into a freestanding circular configuration. A composition of dried flowers can stand directly on a table; fresh ones have to be placed on a plate-like base filled with water. 'The flowers are treated as part of the vase and not just the content,' explains the designer. **VJEMY** studio has invented another 'vase without a vase', which appears to be simply a small wooden table with tubular steel legs. The thick oak tabletop, however, hides a deep glass vessel for flowers.

This page:
**Lambert Rainville • Canada**
'Crown' vase · 2013

Opposite:
**VJEMY • Czech Republic**
'Table for a Flower' vase
· 2011

Jug-like forms inspired **Roger Arquer** to create a minimalist glazed ceramic vase with an additional opening on the side in the form of a funnel, which makes it possible to replace the water without removing the flowers. The pitcher 'Truncus', one of four interlocking ceramic vessels from **Stoft Studio**'s 'Biophilia' vase collection, takes a similar form. Each of the vessels, made from a combination of stoneware, porcelain and earthenware in a variety of shapes and sizes, has been designed to symbolize a step in a plant's growing process. They can be stacked inside one another or used separately.

**Above:**
**Roger Arquer • Spain/UK**
'Funnel Vase' for Danese
Milano · 2016

**Below:**
**Stoft Studio • Sweden**
'Biophilia' vases · 2015

'Fiducia' by **Louise Campbell** is a playful collection of interconnected vases and candlesticks. Individual elements can be joined in many different combinations thanks to magnets located in the vessels' side 'arms'. Produced in glazed faience, they have simple, even naïve shapes. According to manufacturer Kähler Design, 'Fiducia is the Italian word for "trust", and this also characterizes these vases and candlesticks: they belong together as a family and cannot stand alone.' Flowers lit by candles placed alongside them in these charming vessels create a lovely atmosphere.

This page:
Louise Campbell
• Denmark/UK
'Fiducia' collection for
Kähler Design · 2007

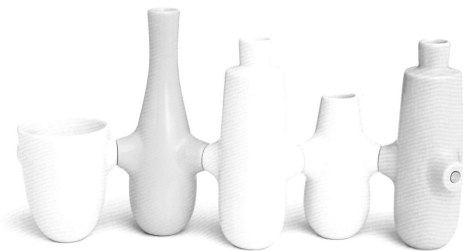

**Louise Campbell**

Matteo Cibic • Italy
'VasoNaso' · 2016

Designer **Matteo Cibic** and ceramicist **Éric Hibelot** have approached vase design as an epic, yet playful, creative process. Cibic engaged in a 366-day research project in which he created a vase every day. Each was unique in style, colour and shape, and all were then meticulously catalogued. The project began as a joke, says Cibic, but 'then turned into an analysis of groups of objects, interpreted as if they were genealogical strains, joined by somatic features, and similar character or colour'. Hibelot has been developing his 'Bidons, Bidons' series for several years as a humorous response to mass-produced containers. Each bottle is unique and handmade, and Hibelot decorates them in joyful patterns, employing mostly primary colours and geometrical shapes. Some have writing on the outer surface, which references – not without irony – packaging labels.

Éric Hibelot • France
'Bidons, Bidons' vases
· 2011

Éric Hibelot

The human body shapes incorporated into these blown-glass vase designs from **Fabio Novembre** and **Vanessa Mitrani** are both technically impressive and visually disturbing. Novembre fuses two centuries-old traditions connected with Venice – masks and Murano glass – in his 'Murana' vase, in which is impressed 'a face without sexual or racial connotations, able to represent every kind of humanity, a soul for an object that could be casually perceived as a vase', explains the designer. Mitrani's vase features the shape of a human hand stretching into the glass at the bottom of the vase. As the name suggests, it is a reference to Hamlet's Ophelia who tragically drowned.

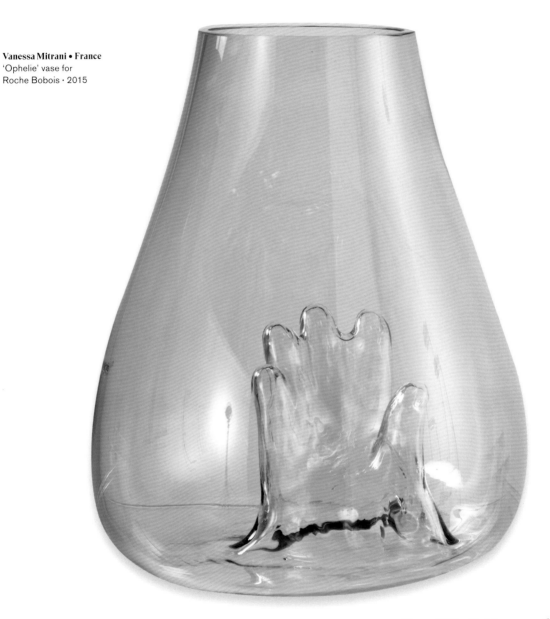

Innovative multidisciplinary designer **Shikai Tseng** turns vases into photographs. The process involves coating the outer surfaces with a light-sensitive glaze and putting the vases into a black box with pinholes (essentially a large pinhole camera) to expose them to outdoor light for 5–15 minutes. Then the vases are developed in a darkroom just like traditional photographs. A reflected image appears on each vase, permanently showing the immediate environment, such as trees or houses, in which the vases were first exposed to light, as if at the moment of their birth. This poetic effect evokes the magic of photographic invention.

These pages:
Shikai Tseng • Taiwan
'PhotoGraphy' vases · 2011

Shikai Tseng

'PhotoGraphy project is the creation of a process in which the environment, time and light react to each other and generate images on three-dimensional objects. (...) It is a new way to capture a moment in time, no matter whether the image on the object is focused or losing focus.' Shikai Tseng

**Shikai Tseng**

Light features unexpectedly in these two vases. 'Life 01' by **Paul Cocksedge** is a deceptively simple-looking crystal vase equipped with a mechanism that uses the flower stem to conduct electricity, activating a light source in the base. So long as the flower blooms the light is bright, but once it starts to wilt, the light becomes weaker. The 'Mummy Vessels' from **Marcel Sigel** are made of spirally wound recycled plastic bags of varying thickness and transparency. The watertight vases are designed to be backlit if holding flowers; empty, they can be used as lamps, lit from inside with supplied small LEDs. Both modes create interesting visual effects as the light shines through the irregularly transparent plastic.

**Paul Cocksedge • UK**
'Life 01' vase for Flos
· 2009

**Marcel Sigel • Australia**
'Mummy Vessels' for smh
· 2005

**Marcel Sigel**

This page:
**Tuomas Markunpoika**
• Finland/Netherlands
'Amalgamated' vases · 2014

**'Pencils are extensions of our minds which enable us to transmit information through different mediums and time, collecting knowledge and creating it.'**

Tuomas Markunpoika

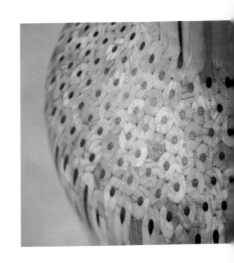

In collaboration with Gallery FUMI and Faber-Castell, **Tuomas Markunpoika** created a set of three different limited-edition vases celebrating the beauty of the pencil. The hexagonal pencils were glued facet-to-facet forming a solid block that could be shaped into a vase by a lathe. The finished vases display striking patterns formed by the pencil leads, seemingly melted into the wood. **Fernando Brízio**, on the other hand, was inspired by multicoloured felt-tip pens, which are positioned so that they leak decoratively onto his white faience vases in different configurations, effectively transforming the vase into a canvas. 'I don't make silent objects,' says the designer, which is borne out by these extraordinary vases shouting with colour.

Fernando Brízio • Portugal

**Above left:**
'Painting a Fresco with
Giotto #1' vase · 2005

**Left:**
'Painting a Fresco with
Giotto #3' vase · 2005

**Fernando Brízio**

A vase can also challenge our visual perception. **Hanna Krüger**'s 'PILA' (meaning 'pile' in Italian) vase for Rosenthal, created by stacking an eccentric selection of plates from the manufacturer's collection, not only confuses the eye with what looks like a stack of dishes in the sink, but also appears to be spinning. **Emmanuel Babled** employs a traditional Murano technique in the 'Cinetici' vase, fusing glass rods to create a rhythmic composition on the outer surface. 'The vertical pattern, composed of numerous glass rods, creates an optical illusion of vibration', reads the designer's description.

**Hanna Krüger**

**Right:**
**Emmanuel Babled • Portugal**
'Cinetici' vase for Venini
· 2014

**Opposite:**
**Hanna Krüger • Germany**
'PILA #2' vase for
Rosenthal · 2014

**Emmanuel Babled**

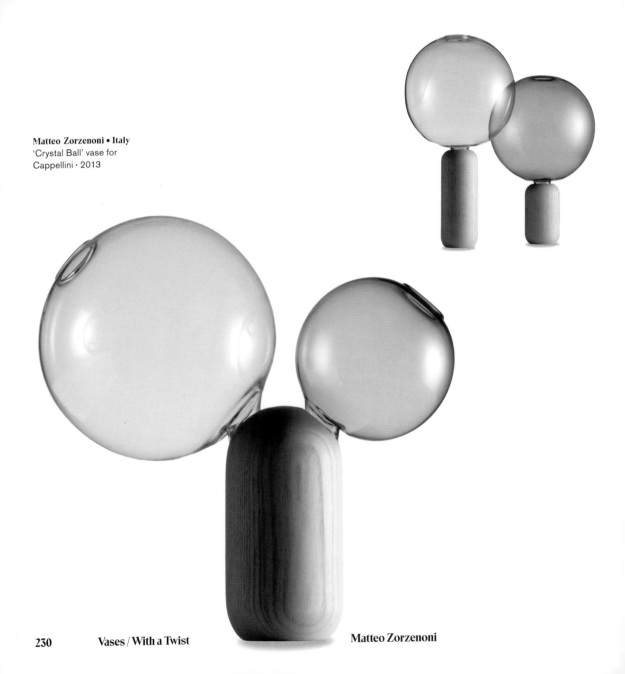

**Matteo Zorzenoni • Italy**
'Crystal Ball' vase for
Cappellini · 2013

**Vases / With a Twist**          **Matteo Zorzenoni**

Designers not only push the boundaries in techniques and materials, but also create vases with playfully fantastical forms. **Matteo Zorzenoni**'s 'Crystal Ball' vases, made from two spheres in various colours and sizes on solid ash or marble bases, was inspired by a childhood game of bubbles. The 'No Limit' vase from **Vanessa Mitrani** is a playful take on a fishbowl (perhaps reminding us of the pet goldfish we had as children). The bulbous vase in blown transparent glass is complemented by a coloured porcelain fish, which appears to be transcending the confines of the glass.

**Vanessa Mitrani • France**
'No Limit' vase for Roche Bobois · 2016

**Vanessa Mitrani**

**Rosenthal Creative Center**

**Right:**
'Pacco Bello' vase
('do not litter' series)
for Rosenthal · 1996

**Far right:**
'Crazy Can' vases
('do not litter' series)
· 1996

**Opposite:**
**Maxim Velčovský**
● **Czech Republic**
'Waterproof Metallic'
vases for Qubus · 2015

Two humorous 'Pop art' vases from **Rosenthal Creative Center**'s 'do not litter' series masquerade as discarded objects, namely an empty milk carton and a crushed drinks can. The plain white porcelain puts the focus on their unusual shapes, and on the unexpected transformation of 'trash' into refined decorative objects. **Maxim Velčovský** similarly makes a luxury vase out of what appears to be a discarded ordinary object, in this case a wellington rubber boot rendered in porcelain with a blue, silver or gold metallic finish drawing attention to its beautiful, gentle curves. The vase concept is playfully ironic: what usually protects us from water now holds it.

Maxim Velčovský

**Right:**
**Adrien Rovero • Switzerland**
'Borderline' vase for
Attese Edizioni · 2009

**Opposite:**
**Apparatu • Spain**
'Terrasse' vase · 2014

Adrien Rovero's 'Borderline' vase is meant for places where we would not expect to display a vase, such as a bookshelf or table edge, thanks to a screw-clamp at the base. This also facilitates the innovative upside-down form, as the narrow base does not actually have to support the vase. **Apparatu** explores innovative mechanical solutions in its 'Terrasse' vase, which has its own water-circulation cycle. Water poured into the vase seeps through the hand-turned unfinished terracotta until it coats the exterior, 'glazing' the surface and sealing in moisture for longer. The vase is equipped with a porcelain saucer to protect the display surface from water.

**Apparatu**

**Itay Ohaly** is a specialist at hiding things below the surface. His collection of three differently shaped 'Black Etched Vases' was inspired by scratch-art childhood craft projects. The vases are covered with several layers of coloured and then black paint, separated by an oil layer. A sharp point can be used to etch drawings into the black surface, revealing the bright colours underneath. In these sample finished examples, the designer has covered a set of vases completely with irregular, doodle-like drawings. The 'Unpacking' project goes even further in requiring the product owner to reveal the final vase. Ohaly uses polystyrene packaging as the actual mould for the product. Resin is poured into the mould, which is then left in place until the customer removes it, revealing the finished vase for the first time.

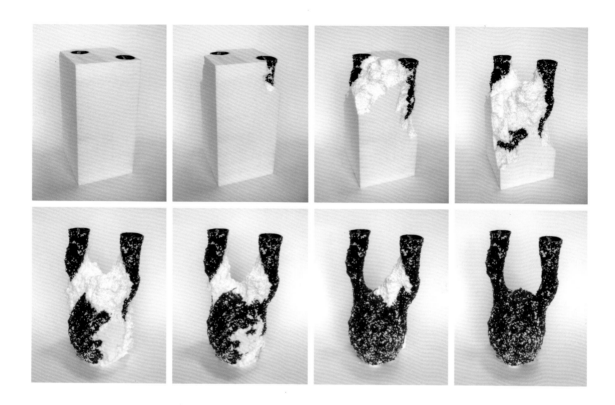

**Itay Ohaly • Israel**

**This page:**
'Unpacking' vase · 2010–13

**Opposite:**
'Black Etched Vases'
· 2015

# DESIGNERS A-Z

# Designers A–C

Page numbers in *italic* refer to images.

## A

**Alvar Aalto  7, 32, *32***
Legendary Finnish architect and designer (1898–1976).
alvaraalto.fi

**Alnoor Design  119, *119***
Paris-based designer Alnoor is of Indian origin and works with many luxury brands and manufacturers.
alnoordesign.com

**Tadao Ando  100, *100***
Noted Japanese self-taught architect, winner of the Pritzker Prize in 1995.
tadao-ando.com

**Apparatu  114, *114*, 115, 184, *184*, 235, *235***
The Mañosa's family-run Spanish design and ceramic studio.
apparatu.com

**Apparatus Studio  88, *88***
New York-based design studio specializing in lighting, furniture and objects.
apparatusstudio.com

**Anders Arhøj  62, *62***
Interior and design studio originally founded by Anders Arhøj in Tokyo in 2006, and which is now based in Copenhagen..
arhoj.com

**Roger Arquer  216, 216**
The Barcelona-born and London-based design teacher and designer founded his own practice in 2005.
rogerarquer.com

**AZ&MUT  104, *104*, 105, 201, *201***
Parisian design company established in 2006 by Rafaële David and Géraldine Hetzel.
az-et-mut.fr

**François Azambourg  186, *186***
Award-winning designer and inventor who is one of the leaders in the French design scene.
azambourg.com

## B

**Ferréol Babin  36, *37***
French designer who produces unique pieces in a number of mediums and also works in industrial design.
ferreolbabin.fr

**Emmanuel Babled  34–35, *35*, 122, 123, 153, *153*, 228, *229***
Lisbon-based founder and director of a creative design consultancy producing furniture, lighting and decorative objects.
babled.net

**Aldo Bakker  123, *123***
Amsterdam-based designer who set up his own studio in 1994 specializing in furniture and product design.
aldobakker.com

**Marta Bakowski  116, *117***
Product designer who founded her own studio in her home city of Paris in 2013 after working for Hella Jongerius in Berlin.
martabakowski.com

**Linda Bayon  102, *102***
Co-founder of Traits d'Union Design studio, French designer Bayon also works independently with various design agencies and luxury brands.
traitsduniondesign.com
lindabayon.com

**Giuseppe Bessero Belti  208, *209***
Italian-born designer who has worked in Milan, London, Paris and now Hamburg, producing everything

from luxury design to electronics
and experimental projects.
**gbessero.com**

**Dror Benshetrit** 176–77, *176–77*
The unconventional Israeli-born
designer and inventor founded his
New York cross-disciplinary studio,
Dror, in 2002.
**studiodror.com**

**Thomas Bentzen** 48–49, *48*
Copenhagen-based industrial design
studio founded in 2010, rooted in
Danish traditions of functionality
and simplicity.
**thomasbentzen.com**

**Jakub Berdych** 177, *177*
Czech sculptor and designer who
established the Prague-based Qubus
Design studio for glass and porcelain
in 2002 with Maxim Velčovský
and currently produces work
independently.
**jakub-berdych.com**

**Bernadotte & Kylberg** 58,
*58–59*
Swedish design firm established by
Carl Philip Bernadotte and Oscar
Kylberg in 2012.
**bernadottekylberg.se**

**Fulvio Bianconi** 185, *185*
Legendary Italian graphic designer
and illustrator (1915–1996), also
renowned as the inventor of many
innovative glassmaking techniques.
**fulviobianconi.com**

**Lara Bohinc** 124, *124*
Slovenian-born jewellery and fashion
designer whose London studio
produces jewellery, home objects,
lighting and furniture.
**bohincstudio.com**

**Bold** 44, *44*, 140, *140*
Innovative design agency and
research lab founded by William
Boujon and Julien Benayoun
in Paris in 2008.
**bold-design.fr**

**Mario Botta** 126, *126–27*
Internationally recognized Swiss
architect who began his career
in 1970.
**botta.ch**

**Ronan and Erwan Bouroullec**
36, *37*, 72, *72*, 90, *90*, 200, *200*
A design duo based in Paris, the
brothers are famous for their ingenious
solutions and unique aesthetic.
**bouroullec.com**

**Fernando Brízio** 227, *227*
Portuguese designer with an ironic
approach to design that allows
opportunites for deliberate 'accidents'
in his projects.
**fernandobrizio.com**

**Itamar Burstein** 178, *178*
The Israeli designer's practice ranges
from injected-plastic household items
and electrical appliances to high-end
furniture and lighting.
**itamarburstein.com**

# C

**Louise Campbell** 217, *217*
The Danish-British designer, known
for playful and experimental designs,
set up her Copenhagen studio
in 1996.
**louisecampbell.com**

**Cristina Celestino** 208, *208*
Italian architect and designer, founder
of design brand Attico, most famous
for producing lamps and furniture.
**cristinacelestino.com**

**Pierre Charpin** 90, *91*
Renowned French designer who has
run a practice designing experimental

# Designers C–F

furniture and decorative objects since the early 1990s.
pierrecharpin.com

**Karen Chekerdjian**  98, *98–99*
Her design studio opened in her native Beirut in 2005, and has now expanded into a brand for furniture and spaces.
karenchekerdjian.com

**Jiwon Choi**  160, *160*
Seoul-born jewellery and accessories designer living between Los Angeles, New York, Milan and Geneva.
jiwonchoi.com

**Matteo Cibic**  218, *219*
Italian designer whose creative company develops products and concepts for manufacturers, collectors and institutions.
matteocibicstudio.com

**Claesson Koivisto Rune**  19, *19*
Swedish architecture and design partnership founded in Stockholm in 1995 by Mårten Claesson, Eero Koivisto and Ola Rune.
claessonkoivistorune.se

**Paul Cocksedge**  224, *224*
London-based studio founded by Paul Cocksedge and Joana Pinho in 2004,

working on everything from product design to architectural projects.
paulcocksedgestudio.com

**Joe Colombo**  120, *121*
Renowned Italian modernist industrial designer, painter and sculptor (1930–1971) who ran an interior design and architectural practice from 1962 until his early death.

**Phil Cuttance**  66–67, *66–67*
Designer and maker from New Zealand, based in London since 2009, known for handmade objects in cast resin.
philcuttance.com

**Jean-Christophe Clair**  70, *70*
French designer and creative director of longstanding Italian ceramics firm Rometti.
https://www.rometti.it

# D

**Kristina Dam**  162, *162–63*
Danish graphic designer and architect who founded her studio in 2012, focusing on furniture, art prints, illustrations and sculpture.
kristinadam.dk

**Lorenzo Damiani**  146, *147*
Italian designer known for furniture and home accessories in both metal and marble.
lorenzodamiani.net

**Sandra Davolio**  14, *15*
Italian-born ceramicist, based in Copenhagen since 1974, specializing in vase designs inspired by nature.
sandradavolio.dk

**Dechem Studio**  50, *50*
Studio founded in Prague by Michaela Tomišková and Jakub Jandóurek in 2012, known for minimalist lighting and decorative objects using traditional Czech glass techniques.
dechemstudio.com

**Paolo Dell'Elce**  154, *154*
Industrial designer based in Milan specializing in furniture, lighting and product design.
paolodellelce.com

**Guillaume Delvigne**  96–97, 97, 106, *106–09*, 109
The French designer founded his eponymous studio in 2011 and has been a member of design collective Dito since 2006.
guillaumedelvigne.com

**Design By O**  34, *34*
Paris-based design studio
experimenting with materials.
**designbyo.fr**

**DIMORESTUDIO**  63, *63*
Established by Emiliano Salci and
Britt Moran in 2003, the Milan-based
studio fuses design, art, architecture
and fashion.
**dimorestudio.eu**

**Tom Dixon**  *6, 7, 20, 20–21, 80,
80–81*
A restless innovator working mainly
in lighting, accessories and furniture,
the British designer created his
own brand in 2002.
**tomdixon.net**

**Jean-François D'Or**  150, *150*
Based in Brussels, he opened
his industrial design studio
Loudordesign in 2003.
**loudordesign.be**

**Sophie Dries**  114, *114*
A young French architect based in
both Paris and Rome, she started
a design studio in 2014 and has
since collaborated with major luxury
interior design and architecture firms.
**sophiedries.com**

**Dubokk**  212, *213*
Copenhagen-based creative studio
designing 'furniture, objects and
everything in between'.
**dubokk.dk**

**Noé Duchaufour-Lawrance**  61, *61*
French designer of ingenious objects
and environments, working in a wide
range of disciplines and materials.
**noeduchaufourlawrance.com**

# E

**Anna Ehrner**  74, *75*
Swedish designer known for her
experimental glassmaking techniques
to obtain unusual colour effects.

**Kjell Engman**  154, *155*
Swedish glass artist who has
designed pieces for Kosta Boda
since 1978.
**jellengman.com**

**Jomi Evers**  *24–25, 24–25*
Norwegian cabinetmaker, product
designer and ceramicist based in
Oslo, he develops and produces
furniture and products both
commercially and as an artisan.
**jomi.no**

# F

**Antonio Facco**  71, 71
A young Italian designer who develops
interiors, products, graphics and
photography, and collaborates with
leading architects and design firms.
**antoniofacco.com**

**Michal Fargo**  *12–13*, 26, *26*
Israeli-born London-based ceramicist
who enjoys pushing the boundaries
of materials and experimenting with
textures.
**michalfargo.com**

**Jean-Baptiste Fastrez**  22, *22*
French designer who established
his Paris-based practice in 2011
and works on product and space
design.
**jeanbaptistefastrez.com**

**Antonio Forteleoni**  *164–165*, 165
Italian interior and product
designer known his for interesting
interpretations of traditional forms.
**antonioforteleoni.com**

**Tina Frey**  64, *64*
San Francisco-based designer
specializing in modern works
in resin and metal.
**tinafreydesigns.com**

# Designers F–J

**Front Design**  *166–67*, 167, *174–75*, *175*, 182, *182*
Swedish practice established by Sofia Lagerkvist and Anna Lindgren, creating home accessories, textiles, lighting and furniture (including robotic pieces and a range 'inspired by their fascination with magic').
**frontdesign.se**

**Studio Furthermore**  *38–39*, *39*
Founded in London in 2015 by Marina Dragomirova and Iain Howlett, working with a 'craft-centric design method', producing furniture, ceramics and lighting.
**studiofurthermore.com**

# G

**Frank Gehry**  134, *135*
Renowned Canadian-born architect and 1989 Pritzker laureate who is based in Los Angeles and famed for many iconic museums, centres and concert halls.
**foga.com**

**Yiannis Ghikas**  180, *180–81*
Greek designer, with a background in computer science, whose work combines functionality and emotive potential in furniture, accessories and lighting.
**yiannisghikas.com**

**Christian Ghion**  205, *205*
Award-winning French designer whose studio has operated since 1998, collaborating with many renowned manufacturers and architects.
**christianghion.com**

**Glithero**  31, *31*
London-based firm founded by British designer Tim Simpson and Dutch designer Sarah van Gameren creating textile, paper and ceramic products, as well as furniture and art installations.
**glithero.com**

**Stine Goya**  134, *134*
Danish fashion designer who founded her brand in 2005 and has a brilliant eye for colour combinations and prints.
**stinegoya.com**

**Benjamin Graindorge**  210, *210*
Young French designer who explores a wide range of materials and products in collaboration with manufacturers and galleries.
**benjamingraindorge.fr**

**Paweł Grobelny**  204, *204*
Polish designer, exhibition curator and lecturer known for both his urban furniture and his promotion of Polish design.
**pawelgrobelny.com**

**Charlie Guda**  211, *211*
Arnhem-based Dutch designer focusing on product design.
**charlieguda.nl**

# H

**The Haas Brothers**  *9–10*, 10
Los-Angeles based multidisciplinary studio run by twin brothers Simon and Nikolai Haas.
**thehaasbrothers.com**

**Alfredo Häberli**  206, *206*
Award-winning designer, born in Buenos Aires and based in Zurich, whose studio produces a wide range of products, including furniture, textiles, flooring, homewares and architecture, for leading brands.
**alfredo-haeberli.com**

**Zaha Hadid**  7, 42, *42–43*, 101, *101*, *128–29*, 158, *159*
Dame Zaha Hadid (1950–2016) was

an Iraqi-British architect who in 2004 became the first woman to receive the Pritzker Architecture Prize.
**zaha-hadid.com**

**Simon Hasan  158, *158***
London-based designer who makes furniture, vessels and objects using the processes of both ancient crafts and industrial design.
**simonhasan.com**

**Hattern  84, *85***
An emerging Korean product brand art-directed by Jae Yang for the firm UMZIKIM, based in Seoul and Milan.
**hattern.com**

**Sebastian Herkner  104, *104*, 152, *153***
German designer who established his Offenbach am Main studio in 2006, woring in product design, interior design and exhibitions.
**sebastianherkner.com**

**Olivier van Herpt  170, *170***
Young Dutch designer pushing the limits of existing 3D-printing technologies to produce sculptures and vessels in plastic, ceramic and even beeswax.
**oliviervanherpt.com**

**Pepe Heykoop  194, *194–95***
Amsterdam-based designer who established his studio in 2009, creating furniture, homewares and collectibles with a focus on recycled materials, and retail products that are made by residents of Mumbai slums via the Tiny Miracles Foundation.
**pepeheykoop.nl**

**Éric Hibelot  219, *219***
French designer and co-founder of contemporary ceramics firm L'Atelier des Garçons, which is located in Saint-Amand-en-Puisaye, a traditional potters' village in Burgundy.
**latelierdesgarcons.com**

**Hallgeir Homstvedt  189, *189***
Oslo-based designer whose studio, established in 2009, focuses on furniture, interiors and industrial design.
**hallgeirhomstvedt.com**

**Robin van Hontem  *172–73*, 186, *187***
Dutch freelance designer specializing in graphic, web and product design, based in Maastricht.
**robinvanhontem.com**

# I

**Ilot Ilov  70, *70***
Berlin-based design collective founded by Ania Bauer, Jacob Brinck, Lena Hirche and Ramon Toshiro Merker in 2006.
**llotIlov.de**

# J

**Hella Jongerius  *190–91*, 191**
The Dutch designer's firm Jongeriuslab has headquarters in Utrecht and a studio in Berlin, and is renowned for research on colours, materials and textures, producing interiors, furniture, objects and textiles.
**jongeriuslab.com**

**Joogii  *54–55*, 56–57, *57*, 84, *84***
Los Angeles-based product and furniture design studio founded by husband and wife team Diogo and Juliette Felippelli in 2015 combining influences from art, fashion and music.
**joogiidesign.com**

**Éric Jourdan  116, *116***
Paris-based designer with a special interest in classic modernist furniture.
**ericjourdan.fr**

# Designers K–O

## K

**Chris Kabel  212, *212***
Dutch designer who started his Rotterdam-based practice in 2002, working with design labels, architects, cultural institutions and galleries.
**chriskabel.com**

**Yukihiro Kaneuchi  168, *168***
Young Japanese product and graphic designer with a background in art and architecture and a focus on innovative products, furniture and tableware.
**yukihirokaneuchi.com**

**KLEIN& SCHÖN  30, *30***
Melbourne-based studio producing handmade, 100% unique creations including vessels and jewellery.
**kleinandschon.com**

**Kókili Projects  199, *199***
A partnership between architect-designers So Jung Lee, currently located in New York, and Gregory Walker, based in Atlanta, making tableware, furniture and home accessories.
**kokiliprojects.com**

**Krafla  198, *198***
An emerging design brand established by Paulina Pająk and Kasia Zaręba, working between Poland and the Netherlands.
**krafla.eu**

**Hanna Krüger  228, *228***
German designer who established her Kassel-based studio in 2011, making furniture, homeware and lighting.
**hannakrueger.de**

## L

**Arik Levy  141, *141***
Israeli-born artist, technician, photographer, designer and filmmaker who has a multi-disciplinary studio based in Paris.
**ariklevy.fr**

**Tomáš Libertíny  45, 45**
Slovakian-born artist who lives and works in Rotterdam and has a background in engineering, painting, sculpture and design.
**tomaslibertiny.com**

**Marie Liebhardt  157, *157***
French product designer, currently living in Copenhagen, known for her minimalist objects and her artistic exploration of flaws and patinas.
**marieliebhardt.com**

**Lyngby Porcelæn  50, *51*, 120, *121***
The Danish Porcelain Manufactory – Lyngby Porcelæn was originally founded in 1936 and closed in 1969. The company was relaunched in 2012, producing many of its classic designs as well as new ones by contemporary designers.
**lyngbyporcelaen.dk**

## M

**Enzo Mari  171, *171***
Renowned Italian modernist furniture designer as well as artist, author and educator.

**Tuomas Markunpoika  226–27, 227**
Born in Finland, the Amsterdam-based designer undertakes projects ranging from industrial design to limited editions and bespoke pieces.
**markunpoika.com**

**Nir Meiri  10, *110–11***
A widely exhibited Israeli-born designer, he established his studio in London in 2010 and creates furniture, lighting and objects, as well as designing interiors.
**nirmeiri.com**

**Vanessa Mitrani** *73, 73,* 206, *206,* 220, *220–21,* 231, *231*
French glass designer who created her first collection in 1998, she currently produces a wide range of objects including glassware, lighting and sculpture.
**vanessamitrani.com**

**Tomoko Mizu** 84, *84*
Japanese designer, now based in Crema, Italy, she founded her studio in 1994 and specializes in both product design and commercial image consulting.
**mizucreativedesignlab.com**

**Ted Muehling** *27, 27,* 28, *28*
A jewellery designer since 1976 with a studio in New York, much of his work is inspired by organic forms and he collaborates frequently with porcelain and glass manufacturers.
**tedmuehling.com**

# N

**Gareth Neal** *128–29,* 158, *159*
Renowned British designer whose East London studio specializes in wooden furniture and decorative objects reflecting the influence of the digital age.
**garethneal.co.uk**

**Nendo** 77, *77*
Design studio established by Japanese architect and designer Oki Sato, with offices in Tokyo and Milan.
**nendo.jp**

**Luca Nichetto** *46–47,* 47
Italian multidisciplinary designer who founded his studio in Venice in 2006, and now has a second studio in Stockholm, designing furniture, lighting and accessories.
**nichettostudio.com**

**Nousaku** 62, *62,* 154, *155*
Design brand celebrating traditional Japanese craftsmanship, founded in 1916, it currently produces mainly tableware and products for interiors.
**nousaku.co.jp**

**Fabio Novembre** 220, *220*
Milan-based product designer and architect focusing on interiors and furniture, he has operated his studio since 1992.
**novembre.it**

**Numéro 111** *118,* 119
French design agency comprising two designers and one architect: Sophie Françon, Jennifer Julien and Grégory Peyrache.
**numero111.com**

# O

**Studio Oddness** *156,* 157
Brand founded in 2015 by Dutch designers Adrianus Kundert and Thomas van der Sman (the two have also continued to work independently), specializing in materials investigation, particularly of ceramics.
**oddness.nl**
**adrianuskundert.com**
**thomasvandersman.nl**

**Itay Ohaly** 236, *236–37*
Israeli designer whose work includes products, systems and spaces, as well as experimental, research and conceptual projects.
**ohaly.com**

**Erik Olovsson** *130–31,* *131,* 142–43, *143*
Swedish designer and founder of multidisciplinary design practice

# Designers O–S

Studio E.O., based in Stockholm, working in product, furniture and graphic design.
**studioeo.se**

**Ontwerpduo**  205, *205*
Established in 2008 by Tineke Beunders and Nathan Wierink, the Dutch design studio is now a close-knit team that is based in Eindhoven and has a mission to 'take fairy-tale ideas and translate them into functional designs'.
**ontwerpduo.nl**

**Anna Elzer Oscarson**  10–11, *12–13*, 40, *40*
Swedish designer specializing in 'patterns and utility goods', she is also the founder of Stockholm-based ceramics brand AEO.
**aeo-studio.com**

# P

**Milan Pekař**  78, *78*
Prague-based designer who established his own studio in 2009 and focuses on porcelain and developing his own glazes.
**milanpekar.com**

**Omer Polak**  *196–97*, 197
Israeli designer and artist who explores new ways of integrating design, science and food experiences.
**omerpolak.com**

**Atelier Polyhedre**  162, *162*
French ceramics studio founded in Nantes in 2004 by Baptiste Ymonet and Vincent Jousseaume, who also developed the CLING brand in 2008.
**polyhedre.com**

# R

**Lambert Rainville**  214, *214*
Montreal-born and based product designer who trained at the Royal College of Art, London, he has collaborated with Nicholas Sangaré since 2008 on interiors and products.
**lambertrainville.com**
**rainville-sangare.com**

**Cédric Ragot**  132, *132–33*, 182, *182–83*, 200, *200*
The multidisciplinary French product and furniture designer, who died in 2015 at the age of 41, is renowned for his innovative approach as one of the international stars of French design.
**cedricragot.com**

**Christine Rathmann**  *82–83*, 83
German designer who has been producing furniture and interiors projects since 2009, both independently and in collaboration with manufacturers; she also works in graphic and product design.

**Moreno Ratti**  *86–87*, 87, 147, *147*
A Carrara-born Italian designer who devoted himself to designing furniture, vessels and objects in marble after studying architecture.
**morenoratti.com**

**Aneta Regel**  14, *14*
Polish sculptor based in London and working in ceramics.
**anetaregel.com**

**Louise Roe**  76, *76*
Quintessentially Danish designer who established her Copenhagen-based interior design company in 2010, making home accessories, furniture, lighting and textiles.
**louiseroe.dk**

**Rosenthal Creative Center**  232, *232*
Design studio founded by the eponymous German porcelain brand in 1961 to develop new projects with

esteemed artists and designers.
**rosenthal.de**

**Adrien Rovero**  *2, 60, 60, 234–35*, **235**
Swiss designer specializing in furniture, lighting and exhibition design, he opened his studio in Renens in 2006.
**adrienrovero.com**

**Studio R7B**  **41,** *41*
Danish designers Mette Bache and Barbara Bendix Becker formed their design duo R7B in Copenhagen in 1996, initially specializing in textiles and now working more widely in ceramics.
**r7b.dk**

**Studio R S W**  *112–13*, **113**
Hanover-based product design studio and consultancy, formerly known as DING3000, established in 2005 by Sven Rudolph, Carsten Schelling and Ralf Webermann.
**rudolphschellingwebermann.com**

# S

**Scholten & Baijings**  *192–93*, **193**
Amsterdam-based design studio

of Stefan Scholten and Carole Baijings, founded in 2000, working in product, furniture, graphic and exhibition design.
**scholtenbaijings.com**

**Héctor Serrano**  **49,** *49*
The Spanish-born designer's London studio was founded in 2000, focusing on product design and spaces (the latter under the name Borealis).
**hectorserrano.com**
**borealisagency.com**

**Marcel Sigel**  **224,** *224–25*
Australian designer of lighting, objects and furniture; formerly senior designer at Tom Dixon, he established his own practice in 2012, based in London and Sydney.
**marcelsigel.com**

**Skogsberg & Smart**  **64,** *65*
Company specializing in bespoke luxury home accessories, primarily glass, created by Magnus Skogsberg and Mimmi Smart with offices in Stockholm and London.
**skogsbergsmart.com**

**SNUG.STUDIO**  **68,** *68–69*
Established by German designers Berit Lüdecke and Heiko Büttner, the

award-winning Hanover-based studio closed in 2017.

**Gert-Jan Soepenberg**  *124–25*, **125**
Dutch product designer and interior architect located in Groningen whose work celebrates traditional hand craftsmanship.
**gertjansoepenberg.nl**

**Kateryna Sokolova**  *92–93*, **93, 160,** *161*
Ukrainian founder and creative director of Kiev-based Sokolova design studio, working on furniture, lighting, hardware and electronics.
**sokolova-design.com**

**Studio Wieki Somers**  **36,** *36*, **88, 89,** *202*, **203**
Award-winning studio founded 2003 in Rotterdam by Wieki Somers and Dylan van den Berg, designing furniture, lighting and home accessories.
**wiekisomers.com**

**Ettore Sottsass**  **7, 79,** *79*
Iconic Italian architect and designer famed for furniture, jewellery, glass, lighting and product designs.

**Mattias Stenberg**  **207,** *207*
The Swedish designer's architecture

# Designers S–W

and design practice, based in Stockholm, focuses on residential architecture, furniture, lighting and everyday objects.
mattiasstenberg.com

**Marie-Aurore Stiker-Metral** *52, 52*
Trained in philosophy, she is a talented young French designer of objects, furniture, lighting and spaces.
mastikermetral.com

**Stilleben** *50, 51*
Copenhagen-based store founded by Danish duo Ditte Reckweg and Jelena Schou Nordentoft, who also design for leading brands and produce their own line of contemporary products.
stilleben.dk

**Stoft Studio** *216, 216*
Swedish design studio in Malmö, founded by Jenny Ekdahl, Ola Nystedt and Joel Herslow in 2013, producing 'story-driven designs' for furniture, lighting and objects.
stoft-studio.com

**Falke Svatun** *144, 144–45*
Norwegian industrial designer who established his studio in Oslo in 2014.
falkesvatun.com

# T

**Leonardo Talarico** *150, 150*
Young, innovative Italian designer who collaborates with international brands from his Milan studio.
leonardotalarico.com

**Hans Tan** *178, 179*
Designer based in Singapore, his work, which includes innovative vessels, 'tiptoes on the boundaries between design, craft and art'.
hanstan.net

**Bruce and Stéphanie Tharp** *120, 120*
The Chicago-based husband and wife team founded their studio Materious in 2005, working in commercial product design, with a focus on domestic objects, and on speculative, non-commercial projects.
shop.materious.com

**THINKK Studio** *4–5, 102, 103, 165, 165*
Bangkok-based studio established in 2008 by Decha Archjananun and Ploypan Theerachai, designing everything from desk accessories to furniture and commercial interiors.
thinkkstudio.com

**Renaud Thiry** *203, 203*
French designer, based in Pantin, whose work includes furniture, lighting, design objects and research projects.
renaudthiry.com

**Vincent Tordjman** *18, 18*
Multidisciplinary designer based in Paris who works on scenography projects and exhibition design as well as interior design and furniture.
vincenttordjman.com

**Nicolas Triboulot** *74, 74, 141, 141*
French designer who started his career in 1982 with Baccarat, and in 1993 founded his own design agency in Strasbourg, focusing on glassware and interiors – even ice hotels.
nicolastriboulot.com

**Shikai Tseng** *222, 222–23*
Multidisciplinary Taiwanese designer based in Taipei whose innovative projects include objects, lighting, furniture and even food.
shikai.tw

**Aurelie Tu** *168, 169*
Canadian-born industrial designer (and former cellist) who has developed concepts and products

for international brands in the lifestyle, technology and sports performance industries; her studio, StudioTu, is based in Portland, OR (USA). **aurelietu.com**

# U

**UAU project**  *108–09,* **109**
Warsaw-based multidisciplinary design studio founded in 2011 by two industrial designers, Justyna Fałdzińska and Miłosz Dąbrowski, with a focus on 3D-printed objects and upcycling. **uauproject.com**

**Paolo Ulian**  *146–47,* **147**
Carrara-born Italian product and furniture designer who worked with Enzo Mari before founding his studio in Tuscany with his brother Giuseppe in 1992.

**Patricia Urquiola**  **73,** *73*
Internationally renowned Spanish architect and designer based in Milan, she started her own studio in 2001, creating a wide range of furniture, lighting, glassware, floor coverings and accessories. **patriciaurquiola.com**

# V

**Bertil Vallien**  **52,** *52*
Swedish artist and glass designer, specializing in sand-casting, who has worked with Kosta Boda since 1963 and used to run its Åfors glass factory. **bertilvallien.nu**

**Anna Varendorff**  **151,** *151*
Melbourne-based jeweller and sculptor, founder of the A.C.V studio producing handmade limited-edition vases and other metalware. **annavarendorff.com**

**Maxim Velčovský**  **232,** *232–33*
With Jakub Berdych, he co-founded Prague-based Qubus Design in 2002, focusing on interiors, architecture, installations and graphic design. **qubus.cz**

**Paolo Venini**  **53,** *53*
Italian glassmaker and designer (1895–1959) who was a central figure in promoting the production of Murano glass and founded an artistic glassware firm that is still in operation. **venini.com**

**Michaël Verheyden**  **87,** *87*
Belgian designer and devoted craftsman, who creates furniture and homewares in collaboration with his wife, Saartje Vereecke. **michaelverheyden.be**

**VJEMY**  **214,** *215*
Studio founded in 2013 by Adam, Samuel and Světlana Cigler in Prague with a focus on architecture, interior design, furniture and tableware. **vjemy.cz**

# W

**Marcel Wanders**  **24,** *24*
Internationally known Dutch product and interior designer, creative leader of a multidisciplinary team of 40, he founded his Amsterdam studio in 1996. **marcelwanders.com**

**Göran Wärff**  **23,** *23*
Swedish artist and glassmaker who has designed for Sweden's premier art-glass brand Kosta Boda since the 1960s.

**Guilherme Wentz**  **151,** *151*
A Brazilian product designer based in São Paulo, he founded his own brand WENTZ for furniture, lighting and home accessories in 2014. **guilhermewentz.com**

# Designers W–Z

**Thomas Wenzel**  *188*, 189
Chief designer for the storied
German porcelain firm Königliche
Porzellan-Manufaktur Berlin.

**Tapio Wirkkala**  *190*, 191
Renowned Finnish designer and
sculptor (1915–1985) whose works
ranged from vodka bottles and other
glassware to ceramics, furniture,
public art and even Finnish
banknotes.

**David Wiseman**  *136–37*, 137
Los Angeles-based American artist
and designer known for his lighting,
installations and objects inspired
by the natural world, in porcelain,
bronze and glass.
**dwiseman.com**

**Thaddeus Wolfe**  148, *148–49*
American glass artist, based in
Brooklyn, NY, whose work includes
mould-blown and cast vases,
sculpture and lighting.
**thaddeuswolfe.com**

**Richard Woods**  28, *29*
British artist whose work spans
art, design and architecture.
**richardwoodsstudio.com**

## Z

**Jeff Zimmerman**  138, *138–39*
American glass artist specializing
in organic, hand-blown sculptural
pieces and lighting.

**Clara von Zweigbergk**  33, *33*
Stockholm-based graphic designer
whose projects range from corporate
identities and packaging to home
accessories, products and stationery.
**claravonzweigbergk.se**

**Matteo Zorzenoni**  230, 231
Italian designer and lecturer pushing
the boundaries of materials in his
furniture, lighting, interiors
and accessories.
**matteozorzenoni.it**

# Manufacturers

Alessi *alessi.com*
Baccarat *baccarat.de*
Bitossi Ceramiche *bitossiceramiche.it*
Cappellini *cappellini.it*
Citco *citco.it*
Coming B *comingb.fr*
Danese Milano *danesemilano.com*
Droog *droog.com*
Editions in Craft *editionsincraft.com*
Flos *flos.com*
Fogia *fogia.se*
Georg Jensen *georgjensen.com*
HAY *hay.dk*
Iittala *iittala.com*
Industreal *industreal.com*
Kartell *kartell.com*
Kähler Design *kahlerdesign.com*
Kosta Boda *kostaboda.com*
Königliche Porzellan-Manufaktur
    Berlin *kpm-berlin.com*
La Chance *lachance.paris*
Lalique *lalique.com*
Lasvit *lasvit.com*
Ligne Roset *ligne-roset.com*
Lyngby Porcelæn *lyngbyporcelaen.dk*
Marmo Trilogy *marmotrilogy.com*
Meisenthal France *ciav-meisenthal.fr*
Menu *menu.as*
Moooi *moooi.com*
Moustache *moustache.fr*
Muuto *muuto.com*
Nymphenburg *nymphenburg.com*
Oddness *oddness.nl*

Postformula *postformula.com*
Prempacha *prempracha.com*
Pusterla *pusterlamarmi.it*
Roche Bobois *roche-bobois.com*
Rosenthal *rosenthal.de*
Serralunga *serralunga.com*
Serax *serax.com*
Skultuna *skultuna.com*
Specimen *specimen-editions.fr*
Stelton *stelton.com*
Swarovski *atelierswarovski.com*
Tiffany & Co. *tiffany.com*
Thomas Eyck *thomaseyck.com*
Venini *venini.com*
Verreum *verreum.com*
Vitra *vitra.com*
YMER&MALTA *ymeretmalta.com*

# Picture Credits

**Agata Toromanoff** is an art historian who has previously worked for collectors and galleries. She has curated and managed numerous contemporary art projects and has written several publications including *Chairs by Architects* (Thames & Hudson, 2016) and *Sofas* (Thames & Hudson, 2018) as well as features in the art press.

On the cover: ECAL / Decha Archjananun, THINKK Studio, Thailand, 'Weight Vase' for Specimen Editions, 2011 (*front*); Yukihiro Kaneuchi, 'Ribbon' vase for Secondome and Fabrica, 2009 (*back*)

*Vases: 250 State-of-the-Art Designs*
© 2019 Agata Toromanoff/Fancy Books Packaging

First published in the United States of America in 2019 by Thames & Hudson Inc., 500 Fifth Avenue, New York, New York, 10110

www.thamesandhudsonusa.com

Library of Congress Control Number 2018945304

ISBN 978-0-500-02124-8

Printed and bound in China by C & C Offset Printing Co. Ltd